GIFT AND CALL

Gift and Call

Towards a
Christian Theology of Morality

ENDA McDONAGH

ABBEY PRESS
St. Meinrad, Indiana 47577
1975

First published in 1975
Gill and Macmillan Limited
2 Belvedere Place
Dublin I
and internationally through
association with the
Macmillan Publishers Group

Nihil Obstat: Gerard Mitchell, Censor
Imprimatur: ✠ Joseph Cunnane, Archbishop of Tuam, 5 December 1974

ACKNOWLEDGEMENTS
The publishers wish to thank the following for permission to include
copyright material in this book: *New Blackfriars* (June 1972) for
"Human Relationships, Sexuality and Celibacy"; The Society for
Promoting Christian Knowledge for "On Discerning God's Action in
the World" from *Theology* LXXV (Sept. 1972); and the Thomas
More Association, Chicago, for "Nationalism and the Christian" from
The Critic (March 1974).

Library of Congress Catalog Card Number: 75-19921
ISBN: 0-87029-048-7

Abbey Press
St. Meinrad, Indiana 47577

Printed in the U.S.A.

Contents

Introduction

This book is the fruit of a number of years' work on the Christian meaning of morality. As the sub-title indicates it is an effort to develop a theology of morality as distinct from a moral theology. Taking as its starting-point moral experience rather than Christian revelation, it attempts to analyse this experience and then confront it with the Christian faith of the analyst. How far the attempt is successful and useful the reader must decide for himself. It may help him to do so if I chart the shape and genesis of the book.

The particular approach adopted here and its expression in book-form is intended to complement, not replace, the more conventional moral theological approach (renewed style) which I myself presented in the recent volume *Invitation and Response*. Pluralism in theology is unavoidable today. Pluralism in the theologian may be one of the safeguards we need to prevent the breakdown in theological communication (and Christian community) which a superficial pluralistic every-theologian-doing-his-own-thing could produce. By trying to approach morality for the Christian from two such widely diverse starting-points and with consequent differences in method I at least found the tension bearable, communication possible and understanding increased.

In the early section of the book, entitled 'Fundamentals', I follow through in orderly fashion the analysis of moral experience and its confrontation with faith in Jesus Christ. The four chapters in Fundamentals ought to be read in the order in which they were written. Development from one to the other is close and complex.

The second section 'Particulars' does not follow the same ordered development. It offers a selection of pieces in which the ideas developed in general in the first section are applied to particular areas. The areas obviously do not all coincide with the traditional concerns of the moral theologian. The 'Particulars' were of course only partly chosen by me. They were for the most part tasks given to me in the course of working out these ideas. The pieces I have collected here are ones in which my basic approach as developed in 'Fundamentals' seemed most influential although for that reason exposed to some danger of repetition. I hope that the reader will come to recognise the close connection between the two sections but even more importantly will accept the value and validity of the topics chosen in the effort to examine the interchange between human morality and Christian faith.

In relating these two poles I have been continually impressed by three ideas, those of coherence, illumination and the possibility of intrinsic connection. This was a cumulative experience which developed over a number of years and a wide range of topics, only some of which are included here. I found for instance that a discussion of Vocation, not normally a topic for moral theology, provided a useful illustration of this. In a rather different way I found myself considering the Church with its responsibility for moral guidance as a learning, as well as a teaching community. Most surprising of all perhaps is the conclusion I was driven to in my analysis of Violence, that it was a question of salvation as much as a question of ethics for the men of violence themselves.

Essential to all the discussion of 'Particulars' is the basic approach of attending to the human reality in all its fullness and then trying to understand it in Christian terms. And in both human life and the Christian understanding, reality displays a gift-embodying-call structure where the gift is at the same time qualified by an element of threat-provoking-fear.

The final triumph of gift over threat in the Risen Christ enables the Christian to approach his morality with the predominant attitudes of gratitude and rejoicing. In Jesus Christ he has a eucharistic and celebration ethic.

FUNDAMENTALS

I

Morality and Christian Theology

MORALITY is a dimension of human behaviour, the dimension whereby behaviour is described as good or bad. Theology is some form of systematic reflection about God; Christian theology is systematic reflection about God as he reveals himself in Jesus Christ, and about the tradition in which he came and comes. It might seem odd therefore to couple them together to form the title of this chapter. Morality and belief or faith would seem methodologically more correct as they coincide at the level of experience. Ethics and theology both belong to the category of organised reflection and analysis and so fit more neatly together. And the canonised phrases combining the two ideas are 'moral theology' in the Catholic tradition and 'Christian ethics' in the Reformed.

Neither of the two canonised phrases is sufficiently neutral to describe the theme of this chapter. They might well decide a quite contrary idea, that of deriving an ethical or moral system from Christian revelation. Christian moral theology has been recently taken by myself among others as an analysis of the revelation made in Christ as a way of life. This is possible and helpful, where it respects the structure of revelation and does not attempt to construct a detailed code of behaviour in a primarily legal form. Christian ethics in the Reformed tradition has a rich and varied history also but does take as its starting-point revelation and the normative account of it contained in the Bible.

It is precisely because I do not wish to take as my starting-point the events or teaching recorded in the Bible that I am avoiding the accepted terminologies, although I value the approach which they embody. And the starting-point is indeed morality and not the systematic discussion of it provided in different forms of ethics. It is with morality as it emerges in human experience that I am concerned. And I am concerned with it as a theologian, that is, as a member of the Christian Church whose training and function is to consider various human phenomena and experiences in the light of what he understands of the person, achievement and teaching of Jesus Christ set as they are within what is called the Jewish-Christian tradition and the community formed by that tradition. My concern then is morality as it occurs in experience and not ethics as elaborated by the mind. I shall be trying to analyse not from a philosophical or simply human and finally rational viewpoint but from that of a believer and theologian.

The order of words in the title 'Morality and Christian Theology' is therefore important. One begins with morality as a human phenomenon and subsequently seeks to understand or illuminate it theologically. The human phenomenon has to be given its full value before any attempt is made to interpret it in Christian fashion. And the human phenomenon is wider than the phenomenon of Christianity or the Jewish-Christian tradition. In fact, as I shall maintain, morality is a universal human phenomenon and has to be treated as such. It is this universal which provides the source material for reflection by the Christian theologian as well as by other theologians or philosophers. To confine the theologian in his reflection on morality to the gospels or the Bible would be to restrict his basis of reflection improperly from the beginning. In so far as a system of moral theology or Christian ethics does this it prevents a complete theology of morality from emerging. It falsifies to some extent the Christian understanding of morality.

To guard against such falsification at the level of general approach it is necessary to outline the sources of this investigation into morality, its method, its purpose, and then to indicate how these are relevant to and treated by the Christian theologian.

The Sources

Too often as moral theologians we have yielded to the temptation to use as sources what other people have said and more particularly written. There is a security in being able to report that somebody else (better known and more acceptable to the particular audience, and for an ecclesiastical audience preferably dead) has already made the same point. References of this kind in sufficient number give an air of scholarship and hopefully impress the reader with the breadth and depth of one's knowledge. Sources mean bibliography, books—at best, in Christian terms, the Bible and some of the key Christian thinkers in history. At worst, they mean an indiscriminate collection of authors listed without evaluation. Books, sacred and profane, form an indispensable tool in the work of the investigator into morality. Their value, however, derives from deeper unwritten sources in the human experience of morality.

A return to sources then is vital to the renewal in moral thinking. The sources are found ultimately only in human experience. How they emerge there, how they are interpreted, structured and assessed, these are difficult and delicate problems. The difficulties should not obscure or obstruct the urgency as well as the necessity of grappling with living experience in seeking to understand morality.

For academics and particularly theologians the importance of experience is easily overlooked. This does not apply simply to the field of morality. Wider philosophical, theological and religious issues bear the marks of such neglect. So much conventional religious education and theological discussion has suddenly become meaningless because people could not relate it to their experience of being human. The nerve centre touched by John Robinson's *Honest to God* testified in part to this divorce of 'God-talk' from human talk, which in the tradition based on the Incarnation should never have been allowed to happen. The 'God-is-dead' movement called attention in a more radical and sensational way to this divorce. In one acceptable sense the God of some theologians and believers was dead because he bore no relation to and could not be incarnate in their humanity as they experienced it. God was a concept but never made flesh. The limitations and inconsistencies, logical, psychological and theological in the work of these people should never permit evasion of the problems they raised, and they should be a continual reminder to theologians of the need to take direct account of human experience and not become absorbed in the second- and third-hand accounts which are the best that books can supply.

The experience in question is *human* experience, that which enters into human consciousness at however primitive a level and is in some degree capable of being grasped or made one's own. Not all such experience is of interest here. It might be more accurate to say that not every aspect of universal human experience is of interest here but we are concerned with universal human experience considered from the aspect of morality, of ought or ought not, of right and wrong. More accurately still one should speak of moral experience and not distinguish between human experience and the moral appraisal of or reaction to it. The human person has an inbuilt capacity to react to the morality of the situations in which he is involved. He has some direct moral awareness. It is permissible to speak of his moral consciousness or awareness, his awareness of the moral dimension of his situation and so of his moral experience. Unless this is accepted I do not see how one moves from statements of fact to statements of value, from experience of the factual situation to recognition of its moral demands, from 'is' to 'ought'. Much of the weakness in the conventional presentation of 'natural law' morality has simply failed to take sufficient account of this difficulty as first expounded by Hume and always alive in English moral philosophy. This does not mean that the 'facts' are unimportant morally. They are very important but unless they already have a value or moral dimension and unless man has a sensitivity to this moral dimension one cannot effectively introduce morality from the outside in, for example, a positivist or utilitarian way.

It would be misleading to conclude from this that it is easy to discern what is right in a particular situation by some specific intuition (or in some Christian terms by divine inspiration). Very patient analysis of the situation will often be required before the precise moral demand is uncovered. In this analysis human reflection or reasoning is the key instrument, provided it is seen to include a basic moral sensitivity. The analysis itself may be cast in some acceptable utilitarian form without invalidating my fundamental belief that man has this innate capacity to discern moral values however faultily and fitfully it may work at times. What is of prime importance here is the recognition that an examination of the meaning of morality must start from human experience and even for the more utilitarian approach there is a justifiable way in which one can speak of moral experience or the experience of morality. It is this moral experience which is the starting-point and indeed the subject of this investigation.

It is necessary to specify this experience more exactly. Human experience as human is of course personal, the experience of a particular person. Only in personal consciousness can one discover or experience the moral dimension of human living and human situations in life. And no other person's may be substituted for one's own moral awareness. Experience, moral awareness, the moral judgment and activity to which they lead must be finally and uniquely one's own if the truly human and personal character of morality is to be realised.

This personal character of morality may not be confused with an isolated individualism. The particular person and the particular situation within which he becomes morally aware are not separate, unrelated and unique in the way suggested by some situationists. While acknowledging one's personal uniqueness as a whole and in specific situations, the continuity of one's person and situation can be properly understood only by considering one's community and historical character. It is in community and in history that one becomes a person.

In a way which requires much fuller discussion than is appropriate here, man becomes aware of himself in community —that is, in relation to others. His experience of himself is not only provoked by his confrontation with others but his ability to grasp it as experience, to humanise and personalise it depends on sharing in the tools of interpretation fashioned by the community. Experience is not separable from some categorising and interpretation of it and for this everybody is, initially at least, dependent on the community into which he is born and educated. In his moral experience as in the rest, every man employs the only tools available to him—those of the community. His moral experience is in this sense a sharing in common experience. Otherwise he could never identify and grasp it as his own. He is not of course finally bound by the categories or moral values of any particular community. Inevitably he will, by encountering other traditions and the differing views of others as well as the different situations in his own life, be led to question, endorse, reject or modify his first categories of interpretation and his first moral attitudes. Yet all this occurs within a community context from which he is not only receiving but to which he is now also contributing. In this way, by the personal development of moral sensitivity in its members, the general moral understanding of the community is itself enlarged. For this the person must remain in communication, in continuity, with the community even if his fresh moral awareness goes radically beyond and transforms the accepted one. Such a radical transformation implies a discontinuity but also an undoubted continuity analogous to various kinds of personal change and development from child to adolescent to adult—or to the religious or secular conversions which occur at such a profound level in some people.

For experience one needs time. All experience, including moral experience, has a history. Each man has a history; he is a historical being. The development touched on above takes place in history, demanding a certain continuity in the person from one stage to the next and from one situation to another

B

but allowing for a certain discontinuity also, through more or less profound change.

In all this discussion the interest is focused on the moral dimensions of experience. This may be provisionally described as how one behaves as a human being, in particular towards other human beings. It involves some elementary ideas of ought and ought not, good and bad, right and wrong. Man has a capacity for such reaction in a situation but to develop it he needs community and time. (He needs these to develop his other capacities also.) The capacity for moral experience or experiencing the moral dimension of a situation involves also interpretation of that situation. (Again this is not peculiar to moral experience.) The interpretation depends heavily on his community and historical background but from these a man is able in the course of his life to fashion a personal synthesis which may not be reducible simply to community and historical elements.

By proposing human experience then as the starting-point of moral investigation I am not opting for sheer subjectivism or private judgment or 'every man his own morality'. Community and historical continuity are essential to understanding this experience. And the experience and its interpretation are of a reality which is not created by the subject independently of the rest of the world. His presence in the situation may change so that James will not always be called on to make the same response as John, but there is a continuity, and the discontinuity or difference does not depend on the arbitrary decision of James. So how James ought to respond to the situation of an alcoholic wife or to the moral demands of world poverty may differ from what John would or ought to do in similar situations but we can recognise some elements of continuity in their situations and in the moral demands imposed on them. Neither James nor John may simply ignore the situations. Neither may adopt a solution of the problem by elimination of the problem people, wife or starving multitude. Both are called to exercise some care for the people and to seek in their circumstances some effective means of help. These effective means will be related to the creativity of James or John and so there is room for creation in meeting moral demands. Yet this is not to be confused with the arbitrary decisions of James or John, still less conceived in terms of suiting their convenience. The 'objectivity' of moral judgments need not vanish with the acceptance of personal experience as a valid starting-point.

The stress on experience has been partly in reaction to the kind of examination of morality which starts from systems, religious or secular, elaborated by other people or accepted informally by the community. In attempting to study morality then one may very easily ignore or falsify one's understanding unless one has worked through one's own experience. Too much moral discussion and exhortation seems unreal because it has no base in one's own personal experience but is received from on high in some abstract system of laws or values. By confronting people with their own experience it is hoped to avoid some of this unreality and help them to work through to a personal understanding of the moral dimension of that experience and the standards it implies, as a basis for more personal moral living. The interaction between understanding and living or mode of behaviour distinguishes man as a moral being as he deliberately seeks to understand what he is doing and to do that which he understands.

Moral experience and its interpretation are not chosen merely as reactionary starting-points but as one necessary and obvious way towards understanding morality. And they have not been chosen for their own sake, as an end in themselves, the object of some academic exercise in understanding. The understanding is of interest in and for behaviour, for action. So the purpose of this study is to help the reader to examine his own moral experience with a view to deepening his understanding of it and so developing his moral responses. The understanding should always be directed towards action as well as derived from it. It should be a form of wisdom and not just of knowledge.

Methods

As in any other systematic investigation methods are determined to a large extent by sources and aims. If the sources are
instances of moral experience of the personal kind described
above, certain methods are no longer appropriate. It would be
inappropriate for example to embark on a history of moral
systems or indeed on a comparative study of the systems
currently or formerly fashionable. The value of such studies is
not in question and the systems themselves, embodying as they
do the organised reflection of other persons and groups of the
human experience of morality, may be of great help indirectly.

The method demanded here is one of direct personal reflection on moral experience. The difficulties involved are enormous and the attendant risks frightening. Given the validity of
the starting-point, there seems no way of evading the difficulties
or the risks.

The first difficulty appears as soon as one attempts to specify
one's moral experience. It is not and never could be pure
experience but already classified and interpreted, in a sense
reflected upon. There is a first-level reflection of this kind implied in awareness of the experience in its moral claim. One
remains nevertheless conscious of the moral claim and in a
second-level and further systematic reflection one must try to
understand more exactly its content as it presents itself and its
basis. Then one tries to discern how far this understanding is
the product of accepted and examined categories of thought
and, given this discernment, how far it should be appropriated
as one's own considered stance, as giving coherence and meaning to one's life and behaviour. A final stage might be reached
where the guiding principles so appropriated might be organised into a consistent but open-ended system, whereby one
would have a unified view of how one ought to behave, com-
posed of some central insights or principles, preferably few in
number, and would still remain open to new understanding,
particular and general as one's experience and moral capacity
developed.

It is very difficult to get one's own experience into focus, let alone do the reflection outlined here. It is so much easier to live and think by proxy. So many people want their moral thinking presented ready-made. Ernst Bloch's adaptation of Thomas Mann's dictum that writers are people who find it very difficult to write to the dictum that philosophers are people who find it very difficult to think applies in a particularly apt way to thinking about or reflecting on one's moral experience. If one attempts to isolate and examine what one might call a serious moral decision in one's own life, the difficulties immediately appear. Which decision would one describe as serious? Is this because of the trouble that it caused one or the importance of the issue? Do these two always or often coincide? Which elements in the decision were one's own, born of one's own choice and which were the product of factors beyond one's control? Did these factors operate at the level of one's interpretation of the demand made on one and could this have been somehow overcome? Or did they solely (or also) operate at the level of possibilities of choice? How and why was one conscious of a moral demand in the first place? What would have happened if one simply ignored it? How far did one implement what seemed to be demanded and how far did one deliberately fail?

If one had to ask and answer some such series of questions before or after every moral decision, life would rapidly be paralysed. And this to many people would be wrong or immoral. So such questions cannot be pursued in every situation. What one hopes for in seeking to understand morality in some systematic way is to preclude the necessity for going through such a catechism at frequent intervals. But these moral experiences provide the raw material for systematic understanding and nobody else's experiences can eventually replace one's own in carrying through this reflection.

It remains equally true that one's own cannot replace anybody else's. This places the teacher of (and writer on) morality in a very difficult position. In fact it excludes at the adult level the systematic teaching of morality altogether in so far as that implies the imparting of a body of information about how one ought to behave. But teaching in any field, at an advanced level at least, is less and less regarded in this light. Third level education is certainly becoming more a process of cooperative discovery and so of mutual education than of the informing of the uninformed by the informed.

Such a concept of teaching fits particularly well into the reflection on moral activity which is proposed here. And it will, I hope, be seen later to suit theological investigation equally well.

In order to realise the possibilities of the method, its limitations must be made clear. The 'teacher' (writer) has no direct access to experience other than his own. It would be foolish to regard this experience as particularly wide or typical, giving his reflection on it the possibility of forming the basis of concrete guidance in a wide variety of situations, presuming he analyses it correctly even for himself. His method is not to use his or any other experience as a way of arriving at solutions for others but as a way of encouraging them and providing one model of investigating moral experience for them. His training, ability and dedication will determine how far he is able to analyse his experience in an honest and helpful way. By reacting to and cooperating in his reflection on his moral experience the students (readers) may be stimulated and helped in the task of grappling with their own.

The inevitable limitations of his actual experience and of his capacity to analyse it, make it necessary for him to confront his own experience and reflection with that of the great moral thinkers of history, with contemporary efforts and with the reactions of his own students. From these different sources he extends the range of his analysis and is able to deepen it and check it against people of different experience and greater powers of analysis. So he neglects the great moral thinkers and traditions at the risk of seriously misleading himself and his students.

Such reflection then is always done in interchange with others, living or dead. It is community activity and takes place over a time, in history. How the personal experience and so the reflection on it is qualified by community and history has already been indicated. It should be a sufficient reminder to any moral thinker that his particular approach is not the only or necessarily the best one.

The personal task which this approach imposes on the teacher exposes him in what can be a difficult and painful way. Every good teacher exposes himself to his students in all kinds of ways that may be painful at times for him but benefit them. (The bad teacher also exposes himself at least to the perceptive but not in a specially helpful way.) In undertaking to analyse his own moral experience (and allowing for the community and historical context) the teacher gives himself away in the deepest and widest senses of that expression. At any rate he ought to. There is a danger that in his articulation of his experience and reflection, he will in fact falsify it consciously or unconsciously. It would be very difficult to be honest even if his experience were readily accessible to him, which it is not, and even if he could readily analyse it, which he cannot. Apart from failures in grasping and analysing his experience due to its obscurity and his mental limitations, there will be failures in honesty as he masks or distorts what he discovers. The temptations here are very strong and, being frequently concealed, they will not always be resisted. By continually reminding oneself of them one may hope to avoid their consequences: misleading the students at the most basic level and undermining the only real value of one's teaching activity.

Purpose

The method employed is only partly conditioned by the source chosen. It also depends on the purpose in mind. These three—sources, method and purpose—are very closely interrelated. In one important sense the purpose governs the other two although it would be better to see all three as influencing each other. At any rate in discussing sources and method it has been found necessary to describe the purpose of the exercise. The ultimate purpose is the achievement of a certain practical wisdom whereby one more easily and accurately recognises the meaning and extent of the moral demands made on one in any situation and so is enabled to respond to them more effectively. It is a capacity to understand but with an understanding that seeks realisation in appropriate action. It is developed ability then to know the moral truth of one's situation which can never be divorced from the general commitment to do that truth. Understanding and engagement to do the truth are closely intertwined and offer the best comprehensive description of the overall purpose of moral analysis.

Morality and the Theologian

So far morality has been treated strictly as an aspect of human experience to be subjected to strictly human reflection. The Christian and the Christian theologian may not ignore or falsify this experience or distort the way of reflection. As members of the race they inherit the rich human tradition of moral wisdom which assists them in analysing their moral life. Within that tradition and history, however, they distinguish one strand of experience and accord it special value. This strand is the Jewish-Christian tradition which records the experience of a people in its relation with Yahweh whom they now recognise as the God of all mankind. It comes to a climax in the person of Jesus Christ. And it is the experience of Jesus Christ, his conscious awareness of himself, his understanding of his personal life, achievement and death, which is taken as normative in interpreting what it means to be human and how a human being ought to behave.

The experience of Jesus Christ is regarded as normative because he is believed to have experienced what it is to be human in the fullest way and at the deepest level. This he did because he was completely human and yet aware of himself as the Son of God. At the ultimate level where man discovers himself because he recognises his relation to the absolute, to his origin and destiny, Jesus Christ discovered and realised himself precisely as Son of the Father and brother of all men. This was finally achieved at the resurrection, the completion of the incarnation. This reality of his sonship and brotherhood he was at once able to articulate and communicate to his fellow-men even to the extent of sharing it. It is in the light of this norma- tive expression and realisation of what it means to be human that the theologian seeks a fuller and deeper interpretation of moral experience.

It is difficult to do this without distorting, re-interpreting or diminishing the human as experienced, in a way that would certainly betray the incarnation. Human experience tends to be short-circuited and one of the weaknesses of some theo- logians and believers has been to concentrate on the divine dimension of Christ at the expense of the humanity. (The opposite extreme has emerged much more in recent years.) For the theological study of morality, accepting the human in all its fullness is one necessary starting point. It is this human which is then illuminated by the person, teaching and achieve- ment of Jesus Christ.

This is not the only possible approach for the theologian as I have emphasised already. As there is a pluralism in approach to the human phenomenon of morality so there is a pluralism in theological reflection on morality.

No approach or group of approaches will lead to a perfect systematic theology of morality. Theology itself is open-ended if we view it as the attempt to understand the meaning of God's gift of himself in Jesus Christ as a call to mankind in terms of the contemporary world; and also an attempt to understand the contemporary world in terms of that gift. Theology is, with the community in which it exists and which it serves, always on the way. It is a 'towards activity'. Because Christ himself is the embodiment of that absolute truth which he calls the Father, he remains a continuing challenge to man's fuller understanding. As man himself changes and develops in history he puts different questions and seeks different answers from the mystery that is Christ in his continuing presence to mankind.

Theology then is a 'towards' activity, always reaching to- wards new understanding. This applies in its own sharp way to a theology of morals. How to respond as human beings called to share self-understanding, sonship and brotherhood of Christ, varies considerably as man changes and develops through history. New possibilities are opened up, new demands are made on him. It is the task of the theological thinker on morality to consider these new possibilities and demands and seek to understand them in their genuine humanness now set in the context of Jesus Christ.

The provisional character of theology should make the theologian modest in his claims to possess the truth. It is for this reason that I have sub-titled this series of essays 'Towards a Christian Theology of Morality'.

2

The Meaning and Structure of Moral Experience

I HAVE already suggested that it would be helpful to seek a
theological understanding of morality through an exploration
of the moral dimension of human experience in the light of the
theologian's belief in Jesus Christ. The first and by far the
most difficult part of the task is the exploration of the moral
dimension of human experience. The limitations and dangers
of such an undertaking have already been outlined. In this
chapter they will emerge explicitly as I try to sketch the structure and basis of that moral dimension.

I. The Starting-point: Experience of Moral Call

The starting-point for the exploration is not the development
of the child as a moral being. That is now, at least for the
writer, shrouded in the mists of the past. Neither is it the
particular moral values nor the system of values or laws or
whatever, whereby one attempts to guide one's moral choices.
These clearly belong to the moral dimension of one's experience. They enter into the recognition of this experience itself,
because, as pointed out earlier, moral or any other experience
does not come raw or uncategorised, but in some elementary
form dependent on the moral categories of one's community.
Yet values or systems of moral criteria do not appear to me as
primary in the experience I wish to explore here. They emerge

at a level of analysis and reflection which is subsequent to the experience of moral call or obligation with its consequent acceptance or refusal, a call which occurs for all of us in actual situations. The moral dimension in one's experience of the actual situation, which impinges on one first of all as challenge, obligation or call, duty or command, provides a useful starting-point, as one can check on it in the actual situation in which one finds oneself. The different words : obligation, call, duty, command, plus others, can express different nuances of meaning or appear more apt to different persons or in different situations. The basic experience is, I believe, the same. For reasons that will appear later I prefer the word 'call' but will use 'obligation' interchangeably with it at this stage as it is more commonly accepted.

II. The Situation

The obligation or call is experienced in a particular situation. Contrary to the assumption of some 'situationists', it is not always easy to define the exact limits of the situation. In the sense that one experiences morality in its basic form as obligation or call in situations, one can fairly describe morality as situational and use the situation as the starting-point for further reflection on the experience. The 'moral situation' is not a peculiar type of human situation any more than the 'moral experience' is a peculiar type of human experience. There is a moral dimension, more or less important, more or less evident, in all human situations and one's experience of them. In the situation of writing this book I may not attend consciously to this moral dimension but various aspects of it may be quickly invoked. There is my undertaking to write a book on a particular topic; my promise to the publisher to have it ready at a particular time (the failure to do that qualifies my further obligation but does not remove it); my obligation to the reader to present my understanding of the structure and basis of morality as honestly, as carefully and as intelligibly as I can; my professional obligation as a moral theologian to make some contribution to a Christian understanding of morality; my general obligation as a human being and Christian to pursue and communicate the truth in the life-situation in which I find myself. Some of these are derivative obligations from a personal undertaking or professional commitment. They specify the more general commitment for me. The relation between these different aspects will require further study but here I am concerned with calling attention to them as forming the moral dimension of the immediate situation at my desk in which I find myself. And some such implicit moral dimension occurs in every human situation; in every situation in which the human being finds himself. It may be more or less important. The clarity, for instance, with which I am called to express myself evidently applies more rigorously to the working out and ordering of my thoughts and to my use of words than to my use of the typewriter or pen; a totally illegible typescript or manuscript would of course frustrate the whole attempt to respond to my obligation and so legibility does form a subordinate part of that obligation.

I stress the *human* quality of this situation. I do not presume to offer a definitive view on similar situations and experiences among ants or fish, still less trees and stones. The recent fascinating ethological studies on animal behaviour will, I am sure, be quite illuminating for our understanding of human behaviour. But we have so far no manner of 'talking to the animals' which would enable us to give an account of how they see and define their situations. The remarkable observations of the ethologists are all from without and the meaning given to the signals received is man's meaning. In accordance with my general methodology then, I must stay within the human experience of the situation and of its moral dimension.

THE INTERPERSONAL CHARACTER OF THE SITUATION
This situation as experienced by the human being is particular and concrete, but it is not, unlike my obligations to publisher, readers or the Church, always immediately and directly concerned with other human beings. The contemporary preoccupation with conservation reflects a moral dimension in our

relation with the cosmos and its resources. The moral obligation which one experiences in relation to property is a more familiar example of an impersonal immediate term of moral obligation. In this latter example the mediate personal term is very influential. Because this property belongs to somebody, is of service to somebody, one must respect it. A somewhat similar case could be advanced for the respect of the cosmos and its forces of which we are now becoming conscious. The appeal is being made in the name of the people, present or future. If one were alone in the universe it would be difficult to make sense of the call to conservation. There are some further problems here about how one treats one's own property, about respect for animals and about a call to respect for the cosmos which seem to go beyond the immediate aims of the conservationists and which require further and fuller elucidation. Yet I believe that not only is the moral experience human and personal in the sense that it is experienced by human persons but also in the sense that its ultimate source as it impinges on one is also personal. The situation itself is interpersonal, although the medium through which the obligation is experienced may be impersonal such as somebody else's property or other cosmic entities and forces as they are related to and available to humans.

In describing the moral situation as interpersonal, as existing between people, whether directly or indirectly, one has to recognise some very important characteristics of the situation, which might easily be overlooked with harmful consequences to its overall moral understanding.

INTERPERSONAL AND INTERGROUP: THE SOCIAL CHARACTER

The personal centre which experiences the obligation or is the source of it may be too easily confined to the individual person. In many situations today where one experiences moral obligation the source is not an individual but a group or society. One has only to think of the feeling of moral obligation towards the victims of natural disaster such as the people subjected to cyclones in Pakistan or earthquakes in Peru; or of the people suffering from injustice, violence, war, for racial, class or ideological reasons in South Africa or South America, the U.S.S.R. or the U.S.A., Great Britain or Ireland; or of the personally handicapped such as the ill or blind or slow learners; or of all those everywhere who are short of food, clothing, housing, educational opportunity, employment opportunity, development opportunity, freedom. In so many places the people involved constitute massive groups from which the moral call to the more prosperous or educated or healthier comes and to which the moral response must be made. Indeed these situations and obligations may be said to be the most important and most urgent facing people in the more affluent countries as well as many privileged people in other countries.

And the situations confront them not just as individuals but as groups. This becomes more evident when one observes that very little response can be made to the situations by single individuals. It is only in organised groups, voluntary such as Gorta, or Oxfam, or statutory and governmental, that any effective response can be made. If such obligations exist and if they can be met only by group activity, then the inter-personal character of the moral situation clearly means intergroup in some instances. And the *subject* as well as the *source* of the moral call is not only the individual but the group.

A sharp criticism of the manual tradition of moral theology maintained that it was very individualistic as exemplified by its concentration on commutative justice at the expense of social justice. This was, in recent decades at least, compensated for to some extent by the development of papal social teaching from Leo XIII to Paul VI. However, the wider and deeper issues of the social dimension of morality as a whole have not yet been sufficiently developed in a systematic way. And one of the great deficiencies here is the deficient understanding of the group as subject of moral obligation and moral response.

The passing attention given to this after World War II in discussing the collective guilt of the Germans under Hitler, for example, did not contribute very much. Its idea of collectivity was under-developed and guilt is not a happy starting-point for fruitful discussion of the moral subject. A somewhat similar critical and negative reaction has appeared in Europe and the U.S. in criticism of particular activities such as the Vietnam War. The War Trials of the Americans in Stockholm provide one example of a growing awareness of collective responsibility and collective failure. Yet very little awareness of the need for a further analysis of the group-subject of morality has appeared in moral writing. Social responsibility tends to be discussed in terms of the individual's obligation to society or to the group, which is indisputable and more easily handled. The group itself as moral subject has received little attention. In what I have to say about the interpersonal character of the moral situation I will have in mind the group to group situation and the individual to group (including group to individual) as well as the individual to individual situation. Not all of what I say will be applicable in exactly the same way to each of these situations but it will be applicable. There can be no reduction of all interpersonal moral situations to the face-to-face, I-thou (or -you) situation of two individuals.

Of course the interpersonal situation of two individuals has its own social aspect which will be ignored only at the risk of misunderstanding the situation and its obligation. Each of the personal poles belongs to a social setting which enters into his being and into the call and response which define the moral situation. At the various levels the individual belongs to a family, local community, linguistic group, racial group, professional or working group, age-group, national group, state, etc., etc. All these overlapping patterns of relationships help to make him what he is and at least some will be relevant in the particular situation. If he is confronted with somebody dying after an accident for example, his call or obligation will vary with his professional group. If he is a doctor he will quite clearly have a different obligation from the obligation he has as a bus-conductor. In a quite different situation—say, of a sexual kind—the fact that the parties are married to each other or that one is the wife or husband of somebody else is clearly relevant.

Thus the social dimension of each person enters in but its precise relevance depends on the particular situation. Some situational discussion of morality unfortunately ignores this. To define the situation correctly (never an easy task) the relevant social setting or relationship of each person must be taken into account.

THE HISTORICAL CHARACTER

So far the picture presented of the moral situation has been a static one; group or individual facing group or individual captured in a still photograph rather than a moving film. Of course the situation and the people in it are not static but moving or changing. One cannot stop the world even to focus on one's moral obligations. With his social relationships, both personal and structural, each person is in historical movement. Because this movement is part of his being just as his social relationships are, it is better to speak of his movement or development as historical than to speak of him moving through history. He is a history. And this applies to group as to individual. So in any given moral situation the historical movement of the two poles, personal source and personal subject, has to be taken into account if the situation is to be properly understood. This again is no easy task.

Source and subject emerge from the past and through the present move into the future. The moral situation which arises and the obligations of the one to the other cannot be defined in terms of a momentary or more extended present. To understand the needs of the one, some awareness of how he arrived at this particular stage of development will, sometimes at least, be necessary. So a patient's previous history may be important to understanding and treating his illness. In group terms some understanding of the historical background to the divisions in Northern Ireland, for instance, is demanded of anyone who seeks to heal them. Some urgent needs have to be met without time for consideration of previous history. And the appeal to history could be used as an excuse for inactivity. Yet at the

C

individual and group level some grasp of how the present need developed is necessary, if the hungry or the homeless, the victims of religious, racial or class discrimination, the lonely or the sick are to be effectively helped and not just have their symptoms alleviated for the moment.

Here the further stage in the historical movement obtrudes itself. The need which is to be served may have developed out of the past but it is anchored in an individual or group moving into the future. The service called for them must be directed towards future development or growth. In lecturing or writing about the meaning of morality one must be aware of the historical tradition from which the present understanding of audience or reader has developed but one is seeking to promote a better understanding for the future. The obligation in this situation as in others is directed towards the future.

The past-present-future elements apply to the subject of the obligation as well as the source and so enter into defining the situation and obligation. His previous professional training and experience influence how far a doctor or a moral theologian has the resources, of himself, to respond to a particular call, and how far he should invoke the help of another professional. In any moral situation the resources of the subject which have developed in the past are clearly important in defining a situation in which he will be called on to serve another for some short time at least in the future. As will be pointed out later these resources are to some extent always potential but one has to consider how far that potential can be realised, to meet the needs facing one. So while anybody might in the very broad sense be a potential medical doctor some already acquired medical expertise is demanded in face of serious illness.

The historical aspects of the situation and its personal poles make it difficult to define it exactly. It cannot, as I said, be captured precisely in a photographic still. It is necessary to consider the relevant elements of the past as well as the relevant possible consequences in the future in relation to source and subject, although, as in the social context, relevance is not always easy to decide. This is partly because so much must remain unknown about the past—and inevitably about the future—if any response is ever to be made. Even the doctor with the most detailed case-history realises that he may not have all the relevant data and subsequent developments may clearly show this. In a less controllable and less professional situation the risks of ignorance are much higher. However, in the human condition these risks must frequently be accepted and the situation defined and understood as fully as possible in the circumstances, yet in that open-ended way that permits one to take account of new data from the past, should they appear and unforeseen consequences in the future, should they occur.

THE SITUATION AS MEDIUM

In seeking to describe and define the moral situation one must take into account the relevant cosmic, social and relational, and historical elements of both personal centres, whether individuals or groups. The situation occurs between the personal centres and the call or obligation and the response relate centre to centre at the core of their being. Otherwise it would be my mind recognising the obligation and not me. It would be my hand or tongue making the response, not me. I would be feeding stomachs but not people. In the professional surgical situation, for example, the concentration may be on a stomach but only in the context of response to a person. Stomachs in themselves would not merit such attention. Any decline in attention to the personal context in medicine as in other fields must negatively affect the human value of an elaborate technical service.

For all its basic importance the personal centre does not confront one in any pure form. Constituted as it is cosmically, relationally and historically with a complex series of capacities and needs, which are in turn cosmic, relational and historical, one personal centre confronts another, under some particular aspect defined by the particular situation.

In the situation of writing and reading this book the aspect of verbal communication emerges and is made concrete in this book which in this sense acts as a medium and gives rise to mutual obligations. (In the earlier part of this essay I used a simpler model derived from one's awareness of moral obligation arising from relationship with another in a situation. But the relationship and obligation are always in some sense reciprocal. This reciprocity will receive fuller treatment later. I mention it here as necessary to understanding how the two poles of the moral interchange meet in the situation.) In the moral situation created by writing and reading this book the medium is defined by the book itself and my obligations to the reader, referred to earlier, include careful preparation and intelligible expression with a view to enabling the reader to understand what I am saying, relate it to his own life-experience of morality and his understanding of it in the hope that it may enlarge that understanding. The cosmic elements of the medium of which physical signs or words are the most important, must combine with the social and historical to make sense to the reader in so far as he can be defined or described. The reader in turn owes it to me once he enters into relationship by reading the book, to read it carefully and intelligently with a view to understanding exactly what I am saying and so to assessing its value in the context of analysis of morality at this level. I have to reach him; he has to reach me; but through the medium of the book.

In different situations the situational medium will be correspondingly different. In one type of situation it may be not communication at the conceptual and verbal level but at the sexual level for example. The sex of the reader or writer of this article is not relevant because it does not affect the medium through which reader and writer meet. (How far theology, and to a lesser extent philosophy, as they have developed have a male bias may, I think, be fairly left aside here.) Where the medium is sexual as defined by the situation clearly the sex of the parties is relevant as well as their historical sexual relationships. To be somebody's wife or husband or fiancée or merely casual acquaintance will be relevant to understanding the moral situation characterised by sexual need or call.

The moral situation arises between people but it focuses their conjunction in a particular way, providing, to use a different optical metaphor, a filter for the cosmic, socio-relational and historical aspects of their existence which are relevant. It is important to define situation as carefully as possible because it specifies the content of the particular moral call as obligation.

III. The Moral Call as Unconditional

The specific character of the call as distinct from its content is a certain unconditionality or absoluteness. Again the exact word to be used is hard to find. What I am trying to express is the way in which the moral call impinges on one as a call to which one ought to respond. There is nothing inevitable or unavoidable about the response. One is conscious of one's freedom when confronted by the call. Yet there is an unavoidable character about the call if not about the response, and one is no less conscious of this in exercising one's freedom by responding or refusing. The sense of obligation or oughtness does not take away one's freedom. It presupposes it. But neither can one's freedom dissolve the sense of obligation. For different people and in different situations the sense of obligation, of the unconditional character of the call will vary. It may be increased or diminished. Some types of call will be regarded as unconditional in this sense by some people and as merely conditional, dependent on what one wants, by others. In some situations, as in the case of the driver of a car confronted by somebody lying on the road and feeling obliged not to run over him, the unconditional call seems to arise directly. In other situations, those involving contract or promise or marriage for example, the call is dependent on some relationship undertaken freely and to which at some stage one had no obligation. John might not have married Mary, or I might not have undertaken to write this book. Once one has undertaken, however, certain unconditional calls will arise.

It's important to insist on this aspect of the moral call, in the face of a certain relativisation of morality. This is more commonly understood in terms of a relativity of content but there is a deeper relativity which influences the relativity of content. We are all aware of the differences even in our own culture about practical and important issues like war, poverty, revolution, political dishonesty, tax evasion, advertising, pornography, euthanasia, etc., etc. What is not always realised is that part of the difficulty arises from relativising the moral obligation itself by insisting too much on a teleological model, whether that is salvation of one's soul, the greatest happiness of the greatest number, or some other individual or social goal. To somebody not interested in particular goals, the linking of particular or all moral obligations with them may easily lead to an 'if' or 'conditional' approach to morality. If I wish to attain this goal, I should do this, but only 'if'.

In my view the moral obligation is an aspect of experience which in some situations occurs as something which one may not evade or refuse. Evading or refusing it does not abolish it. It remains with one at least in the sense of judgment on failure. Of course, it is possible to dull the sense of obligation and of failure in some or all areas in which one encounters it. But the moral analyst is primarily interested in the moral reality itself in a clearly recognisable form and in this form it emerges as independent of one's own desires or projections. It constitutes a primary experience which may not be reduced to or produced by some other experience. This is not the place for an extended discussion of the is-ought question or the naturalistic fallacy. My own experience suggests that the route to be taken is from 'ought' to 'is' and not the other way round. One can and should investigate one's experience of ought or obligation or moral call in order to define more precisely its content, to understand the medium and to understand the base on which it rests, that which the medium mediates. The second of these tasks will occupy the rest of this chapter.

In insisting on the unconditionality of the actual and proper moral experience of the situation, in appealing to its primacy as a datum of experience, I am not suggesting that it is some kind of mystical or mysterious experience available only to the few or closed to further investigation. It is a common experience, I believe, and demands further investigation. I do not believe that it is best described as intuition when it is simply an awareness of a certain dimension of one's experience which develops in the course of one's life. It may have, as is sometimes suggested nowadays, certain affinities with literary or artistic discernment. This has much more to do with refinement in deciphering the contents of the obligation than with the experience of the obligation itself and such a model may be very misleading.

IV. Human Otherness as Source

Further reflection on the unconditional call in the situation anchors it very firmly in the personal poles, individual or group which may be described as subject and source. The subject is aware of this call through the medium defined by the particular situation but he is aware of it as coming from the personal source. Through the situation and the call which it articulates, subject encounters source—and encounters source as source of the unconditional call. Whether it is a situation calling for respect for life or property, for verbal or sexual communication the personal source of the call is at the same time source of its unconditionality.

The moral interchange through the medium of the situation between personal subject and personal source (individual or group in either case), has a number of important characteristics. One obvious one, that of reciprocity, may be left aside for the moment while I concentrate on the subject's experience of the personal source in the call or obligation. I stressed earlier that the encounter was between two personal centres and not between a need and a service. In many situations the experience itself sufficiently indicates this: one's obligation and response to hunger or illness are experienced as personal obligation and response to the hungry and the ill, to the persons. In other situations the encounter may be mediated through property or social structures (e.g. voting, taxation) or through some aspects of the cosmos itself but the ultimate term is another personal centre, individual or group.

HUMAN OTHERNESS AND UNCONDITIONALITY

The personal term of the encounter throws light on the unconditionality of the moral call described above. Irrespective of or rather prior to any particular need, the person calls for a recognition and respect that may not be directly explicit but implicit in the particular call and built into the particular situation. Very little reflection will make explicit the peculiar call to recognition and respect which each personal centre embodies. As compared with a non-human, cosmic entity the human person (as individual or group) calls for a recognition and a respect which will not permit one to use (or abuse) this person as simply an instrument and so an extension of oneself. One may not manipulate him as subordinate to oneself, one's possession. One may not indeed possess or strive to possess him or simply eliminate him. He confronts one, calling for recognition and respect with an independence which one may not ignore. Positively this independence makes him a different source of knowledge and understanding, freedom and initiative, activity and love. He is another world. Negatively one may not (and indeed on further reflection cannot) use or possess or eliminate him. He remains *finally other* than oneself. The primary generic call in any situation is to recognise and respect this otherness. It manifests itself through some specific call in the situation and is the source of unconditionality in the specific call.

HUMAN OTHERNESS AND UNIQUENESS

In any situation the subject of the moral experience is personal and so is the source, to be recognised, respected and responded to in the particular demand mediated by the situation. The human otherness of the source, its quality as this different, insubordinable, unpossessable centre of life and knowledge and love, as this particular human world, makes it finally and irreducibly different from the human subject (in its otherness) and all other human centres in the wider community. It makes it in that sense a unique world of its own. So moral exchanges occur between unique personal centres which not only may not, but ultimately cannot, be reduced the one to the other. This final difference or otherness emerges in the actual moral situation as the unconditional or unavoidable quality of the particular moral call itself.

The otherness and uniqueness are of course two-way. They apply to the subject as well as the source. The call emanating from the source is to an irreducibly different and unique subject. The uniqueness of the personal centres or poles in any moral situation gives the situation itself a uniqueness which cannot be denied but which does not exclude it entirely from continuity with similar situations involving other people or the same people at different times. It is the denial of this continuity which makes the otherwise valuable insistence of certain situationists on the uniqueness of the situation ultimately indefensible because it is unintelligible. If there is no continuity between human situations, if they share no common elements at all, then there are no words to describe, indeed no way of recognising them. If the words used have a totally different meaning in each situation one has no way of telling what this meaning is, of recognising what they describe. The love of every husband and wife is different, unique because of the unique personal poles involved. Yet how can one describe John's attitude to Mary as love and Michael's attitude to Jane also as love, if one maintains that there are no features common to both? And how can one describe John's action in a particular situation as loving or unloving if one denies any continuity between this situation and another situation in which one would want to describe his action also as loving or unloving. Continuity between situations and sharing of common elements are implied by the intelligibility of the situations themselves. To deny this intelligibility is to deny one's right to discuss the situations at all and to opt out of all that is called human discourse about morality.

It is not my purpose here to launch into a full-scale discussion of all contemporary versions of 'Situation Ethics'. I felt it necessary, however, to call attention to the uniqueness which undoubtedly exists not only in the moral situation but also in the context of its relation to other situations. The features of continuity with historical overtones, and of shared elements with social overtones, apply not just to the situation but to the personal poles meeting in it. Indeed the meeting of the personal centres in the situation, for all the emphasis that has been placed on their otherness, is possible at all because they have something in common; they are in communion or community and so can communicate with or encounter each other. The otherness exists and emerges within a common bond in some community however elementary. It is the extension of the community, at a very elementary level admittedly, through the communication media, that brings Irish people into contact with Biafrans or Pakistanis and so creates a moral situation in which they experience a call to help these people.

Human otherness within community, within some actual and possible communication, provides the basis of the moral situation. Although it has been treated here from the point of view of subject and source as corresponding to the conscious experience of moral call in one of the poles, there is at this basic level a clear reciprocity. Each is called to recognise and respect the other as other within the community, whatever might be the particular concrete response in which recognition and respect are expressed. We shall have to return to this reciprocity between human others in communion again and again in the further analysis of the moral experience. The concept of otherness for all its importance must not obscure community as the context in which it exists; communication as the method of recognising, respecting and responding to it; communion or deeper community as the crowning achievement of response. Without the 'commun-' dimension, human otherness could provide no insight into the experience of morality. And the 'commun-' dimension seems necessarily reciprocal. To be in community, to communicate, to achieve communion—all involve mutual recognition, respect and response.

V. Other-centredness as Criterion of Moral Response

If we concentrate, for the sake of simplicity, on one of the personal poles in the moral situation, his experience of the moral call to response as emanating from the other through the medium of property or bodily need or whatever, with its implicit call for recognition and respect, reveals the direction of the moral response. It must follow the call in the direction of the other. It must be other-directed or other-centred, if it is to be faithful to the call. To turn back on the self by refusing the call or to respond to the other as a means of promoting the self and so fail to recognise and respect the other as other is what I should call moral failure. The inherent dynamism of response to the call is to break out of the self to reach the other by recognising, respecting and responding to him through the medium in which one encounters him in the particular situation. In brief then, one behaves morally when one responds in an other-centred way; one behaves immorally when one behaves in a self-centred way.

There are very many problems about this which I prefer to discuss later. I may mention that the response in its totality requires time. It has a history. It moves from understanding of the past through the present to serve the development of the other in the future. The historical dimension of the whole situation has to be taken into account and a refusal to give something to the other in the present may be other-centred if referred to the future as so frequently happens with children, for example; just as to give in the present may be self-centred, to rid ourselves of some irritation or nuisance. The social dimensions of the two poles, their various relationships at the personal and structural level, are no less important. And they may lead to even more acute difficulties as one recognises the other in his social setting and the self in his and tries to decide whether the limited resources of the self may be directed to this other for the present in view of one's many different commitments. The family man has to think of his commitments to wife and children when he encounters another in need. Of course his concern for them may not necessarily be decisive in the actual situation as for example when he is faced with some-body drowning, or it may be barely relevant if it is some small or short-term demand for money or care. The social dimension of the other as source of the call applies in innumerable ways also. Recognition of his world in a way relevant to the situation will frequently call for some recognition of his other relationships—that he is somebody's husband, for example, in a sexual situation.

The call one experiences in the moral situation is first of all a call to understand the situation correctly, to understand the other as he encounters one through the particular moral situation in order to respond to it as effectively as possible. Anything less than that kind of recognition is a failure to respect the other as other and ensures failure to make the further appropriate response.

VI. Gift-call Character of Moral Situation

In all this the subject's moral experience of the other in the situation may very easily have given an impression of the other as burden, simply source of moral demand or call. On reflection I think this impression should be corrected to seeing the other primarily as gift but gift embodying call. The world of the other with which one is confronted comes to one as gift in both senses of that expression. He is given : he is not in any sense one's own achievement but freely presented to one. He is present as *present* and in the second sense associated with gift he is present as *enriching* or at least potentially enriching one's own world. Any encounter with the world of another has this potential. Every other man or group comes to one first of all as gift.

The gift aspect has its root in the otherness-in-community already discussed. Human otherness has its biological, psychological and sociological dimensions—the individual genetic code with its physiological and psychological consequences; familial and wider social and environmental factors. The historical interaction of all these contributes to the gift-otherness of the individual human as he confronts his fellow-humans. All these factors contribute to the different individual world which he constitutes within the wider human world in which he exists, is present to and communicates with his fellow-men. But the difference and the irreducible otherness are not explicable simply in these terms. His ability to recognise and organise these elements in the face of all other worlds, personal, social or environmental; his ability in other words to determine his own life and relationships by his powers of personal knowledge and freedom, decision, and self-giving, reveal more exactly how his otherness is at once gift, offering entry to a new world, and call for recognition and respect.

Yet the other is primarily gift, a free and enriching offer. The gift of the other implies offer by him, invitation to enter his world. It is possible only in community and communication. One may not force an entry into the world of the other. But his very presence always involves some sharing, however minimal, in his world. It changes one's own world in however limited a way. It enriches one, in very varying degrees admittedly. The manner of this enrichment will be investigated in detail in the next chapter. It does not take place, however, by seeking such enrichment in itself by a passive reception of the other, or by exploitation or using of him but as indicated already in discussing the moral direction of our activity, by active attempts to recognise, respect and respond to him. This is how one enters his world and is enriched by it. The gift embodies call. As gift it involves a call to move out of the world of the self in recognition and exploration of new worlds. The basic biological, psychological and sociological differences with their personal realisation and transformation in individual social and cultural developments, clearly enrich all of us but their supreme and unique manifestation as *gift* in the people one meets might well be overlooked.

The primacy of the other as gift in the moral situation precludes the understanding of morality or of the other as burden. The first reaction called for is one of thanksgiving for the gift, of celebrating its presence. Indeed the richest human exchanges are of this kind. And the call which the gift undoubtedly involves, includes, apart from any further specifications, a call to recognise the other as gift and rejoice in his presence. In some situations this may be very evident although the common celebration may not be seen as answer to a moral call, with consequent impoverishment of the meaning of morality. If this gift element is not recognised as always present and is not sometimes explicitly attended to, moral call and the existence of others as source of moral call become increasingly and exclusively burden. How morality can degenerate in this way may be traced perhaps in one's own history, in the story of a breaking marriage or, as I shall indicate later, in the story of covenant and Law in Israel.

VII. Threat-fear Character

It is the other as gift who embodies the call and summons one out of self to recognition, respect and particular response. Yet it would be very unrealistic to describe the other and one's awareness of the other exclusively in terms of gift embodying call. The presence of the other precisely as this different and irreducible world of its own may also constitute a *threat, provoking fear.* There is ample evidence of this from every kind of human interchange between groups, whether states or races or classes or religions, and between individuals, even individuals in such ostensibly favourable situations as the family or the religious community or the Church.

The existence of the other as threat may be due to his seeking to eliminate his opposite number by murder for example, or at least to refusing to accept his independent existence, seeking to absorb him (even temporarily) into his own world. Conversely the other may emerge as threat because the self refuses to recognise his existence or sees his independent existence as upsetting his own controlled and controllable world. This is not due then to any moral fault on the part of the other but on the part of the self who cannot tolerate the existence of this separate and independent world. Because he is self-centred and will not recognise or tolerate other worlds except in so far as they are subordinate to his own, their existence becomes threat.

One seldom finds a pure situation where the other or the

self is simply threat. More usually there will be elements of threat mixed with elements of gift on both sides. In daily living the relationship between husband and wife, parents and children, professional colleagues, neighbours, even fellow-religious or fellow-Christians is a mixture of gift and threat. How often has one seen the threat element gradually predominate in a situation which started as gift on both sides whether in marriage or in the Church. The relationship between different groups in the Church today is too often predominantly one of threat-fear instead of gift-call. Theologians constitute a threat to and feel threatened by the hierarchy in a situation where the gift-call dimension should predominate if anywhere. In the teaching situation between teacher and student the same element exists and sometimes predominates. In the business organisation of our world, in spite of all the sophistication of modern managerial methods or Madison Avenue advertising, the underlying element of threat can too easily predominate. It is scarcely necessary to draw attention to this danger at the political level, national and international.

VIII. Ambiguous Character

In the actual and moral situation, whether of group to group, of group to individual or of individual to individual, the gift-embodying-call is always combined with threat-provoking-fear. Given the reciprocity of the relationship and the moral direction of the relationship on both sides as recognition of, respect for, and response to the other as other, it would appear that the moral direction of the call is also towards enabling the gift to triumph over the threat and so towards enabling the genuine communion and mutual enrichment of the two worlds and not towards the elimination or subordination of one or both.

This will not be easily or always achieved as far as one can judge from human experience or morality. And it will take time and patience and effort. Total surrender to threat is no more moral than total imposition of it. It is the transformation of threat into gift and so of the hostile confrontation of different worlds into their developing communion which is the moral task of all men in their different situations.

Conclusion

In seeking to outline the structure and basis of morality, I have taken as my point of departure the situation in which the moral dimension emerges in one person's (the subject's) experience of moral obligation, which I prefer to describe by the wider term 'call'. The other pole (the source) of the situation and the call is also personal, although the relationship may be more or less direct or immediate. And both poles may be personal as groups or individuals.

The situation while interpersonal has cosmic, historical and social dimensions arising from the conjunction of the personal poles which exist in the cosmos, in history and in a network of relationships. Which of these elements are relevant to defining the moral call in the situation will vary with the particular need of the source as expressed in the call and the resources which the subject has to meet it. And while the two personal poles do make contact with each other at their personal centres, it must be through some of the many facets of their personal existence which act as medium and define the situation in some general way, such as verbal communication or sexual endowment or physical health.

The call as properly moral has a certain unconditional element about it. One ought to respond; one is free not to. But as the 'ought' or call does not take away one's freedom, one's use of it in responding or refusing to respond does not abolish the 'ought'.

At this level also the moral call seems to me a primary datum of experience, though it may be misinterpreted or weakened or scarcely developed. And, as with all our capacities to discern some aspect of reality, it develops in some social context.

The experience of moral call in a concrete situation under a particular form, as unconditional or unavoidable, as interpersonal and as a primary mode of experiencing, yields on further investigation the concept of the personal source as finally other. This quality of irreducible otherness is of course reciprocal but in the subject-source model underlies the unconditional call of the source and reveals that whatever the particular situation and particular call, there is always a call to recognition of and respect for the other as other which then seeks fulfilment in the further response to the particular call. This recognition, respect and response are only possible in the context of community, where in other words communication is possible and they are directed towards fuller communion of the different worlds. The moral direction of one's response then is towards the other. If it is a proper moral response it is, according to this analysis, other-centred.

The other does not on deeper reflection confront one first of all as call but as gift. The gift of this freely bestowed and potentially enriching different world of the other embodies the call to recognition, respect and response which leads, as a consequence, to the enrichment of the subject. The gift-embodying-call view of the other and its recognition as structuring the moral situation could have an important liberating effect on one's approach to morality.

However, gift embodying call is not the only way in which the other reveals himself in the moral situation. He can also appear as threat provoking fear, either because he wants to take over one's self and one's world or because oneself will not tolerate the existence of such another independent world. In most moral situations the gift embodying call, the enrichment aspect is mixed with threat provoking fear. And the correct moral direction in this ambiguous situation is towards the predominance of gift-call over the threat-fear.

In later chapters an attempt will be made to follow out this structure in the development of the person through his activity in various areas of human living, with the various difficulties and limits which this involves, before examining the whole analysis in the light of the revelation made in Jesus Christ.

D

3

The Moral Subject

The Subject in Response to Source

IN seeking to understand morality as it occurs in human experience I have had to use as a starting-point my own experience as the only one to which I have direct access. By acknowledging the social origins of that experience and of the categories in which I recognise it as well as by comparison with the experience of others to which I have indirect access in their own accounts of it, I believe that this experience is not entirely eccentric or individualistic and so has some features in common with the experience of the reader. If it is not seen to have any common features, then the analysis of its structure and basis will have made no sense. And even if he accepts some common features in the experience itself, the reader may still find very little that is illuminating for him in the further analysis of the structure in terms of subject-source (individual or group) and of gift-embodying-call combined with threat-provoking-fear, of the basis in human otherness, and of the criterion of morality as other-directedness, growth in communion and the overcoming of threat by gift. I mention these difficulties here in the awareness that my starting-point in my own experience has such very serious limitations that they may undermine the whole enterprise. And yet the risk has to be taken if one accepts that one's experience of morality is one valid way into understanding morality and providing some help to others in understanding theirs. Of course not everybody who starts with his experience will analyse it in the same way. And I could visualise myself analysing or structuring mine in quite different ways. The way I have chosen to analyse it, however, seemed to me, after quite a long struggle, a particularly apt way for me and in this chapter I wish to take it a stage further.

In the last chapter I concentrated on the situation in which the moral call emerges. This is basically an interpersonal situation, a situation involving two personal centres or poles, whether individuals or community groups. To simplify the discussion I referred to one of these centres as the subject who experiences the moral call and the other as the source from whom the call originates. I did, however, insist on the mutuality or reciprocity of the situation itself. Whatever form the specific call as experienced by the subject might take, the underlying interrelation required some mutual recognition, respect and response. If the subject is a doctor faced with a patient in need of appendectomy, the moral call which originates in the patient and urges the doctor to provide this professional service occurs in a context in which the patient has to recognise, respect and respond to the doctor in various ways also. The moral call or obligation operates in both directions, even if one specific aspect, the call to perform the operation, is much more obvious and urgent. The doctor could not normally respond to this call unless the patient cooperated, and where the patient is too young, unconscious or otherwise unable to cooperate, there may be other people involved who present the patient to the doctor and cooperate on his behalf, and afterwards the patient will be called to cooperate in so far as he can. In other professionally defined situations the lecturer and the student, the bus conductor and the passenger, the policeman and the citizen meet each other with reciprocal calls at least of the recognition and respect kind. In situations not so professionally but yet socially defined, such as marriage or the family, or scarcely defined at all, such as the road-accident, the call may, in particular circumstances, be more urgent or obvious for the husband or parent or witness to the accident but the reciprocity is always present. In discussing the moral subject then or the subject of the moral call this reciprocity must be continually borne in mind. The subject, individual or group, is also source of moral call and the source is always subject to moral call. So while X may be the subject most urgently called to respond to Y because of Y's particular need, Y will have also his call to respond to X at least in recognition, respect, gratitude. If one refers back to the key concept of the personal poles as gift to each other, it is obvious that gratitude arises as a moral call on both sides.

The reciprocity of the moral situation prevents us from speaking of one pole exclusively as subject of the moral call and the second exclusively as source. In the fuller terms of the previous analysis, each is in turn gift-embodying-call to the other, to be met with recognition, respect and response. In discussing the moral subject further this must be constantly borne in mind, even if it is at times more convenient to concentrate on one pole as subject. (It must be equally remembered that this subject may be group as well as individual.) However, it is in a situation of interchange that the subject becomes aware of the source as source and of itself as subject. Its awareness of the source as origin of moral call involves at the same time its awareness of itself as moral subject, as subject/recipient of this moral call. The moral situation develops historically through the awakening of the subject to the call emanating from the source, in the recognition by the subject of the source as source and so of itself as subject.

The moral subject's awareness enters into defining the situation itself. This awareness has of course a history, short or long, and it may begin in a very faint and vague way before developing into a full and precise awareness of the particular moral call in the situation. This full and precise awareness is really the conscience judgment. The manner of its development varies from subject to subject and from situation to situation. What is relevant here is that the awareness is ultimately awareness of the source as impinging on the subject through this particular moral call. Within the pre-existing communion the two personal centres are distinguished by the subject as source and subject, and the distinguishing and awareness offer an opening to a fuller and higher communion, as my earlier discussion of the moral response and its criterion indicated. The first task of this chapter is to analyse more fully the subject's relation to the source through the total moral response, beginning from the moral awareness just mentioned. It will at the same time seek fuller understanding of the moral response itself and its relation to the moral subject. In this way it is hoped to avoid some of the limitations of a moral analysis which concentrates on individual actions in isolation from their origin, the subject, and the historical significance of these actions in the subject's continuing history. It is not only the traditional manuals of moral theology such as Noldin or Prummer which tend to discuss 'human acts' in isolation from the historical subject; this is a common tendency also among 'situationists' of the Fletcher kind, as Paul Ramsey for a quite different reason has shown, and leads to some of their unacceptable conclusions.

The primary concern now is the subject-in-response-to-the-source : not just the response and not just the subject. In the first case one would be dealing with actions divorced from their moral-making source and content. In the second case one would be dealing with attitudes divorced from the actions which express them and create them, which make them real attitudes *in* as well as *to* the world—loving, courageous or just attitudes are expressed, developed and recognised by the subject himself through his loving, courageous and just action. A *Gesinnungsethik* divorced from consideration of action is inadequate to the moral reality of my experience at least. It is the subject-in-response and subject-in-response-to-source which is the concern of this moral analysis.

Phase One: Other-recognition and Self-identification

The first stage in the subject's response or the first move of the subject-in-response is his recognition of the other as source of call. This involves, on reflection, some recognition of the other as gift and perhaps threat but such reflection and refinement may be ignored for the moment. The other individual (or group) is more obviously and immediately distinguished through the particular call emanating from him in the concrete moral situation. He (or it, if a group) impinges on the subject through the call expressed in the particular situation. But it is he, the source, who impinges and it is on the subject he impinges, as I emphasised before. Through this interchange the subject and source emerge as subject and source of the moral call. From the subject's viewpoint his recognition of the source as source enables him to identify himself as subject.

This recognition and identification require further elucidation. The presence of the other as source of particular call awakens the subject to awareness of the call, of the other as source of it, of the subject as subject. This awareness is first of all of the very concrete and particular call emanating from the source—to feed the hungry, to care for the sick, to liberate the enslaved, to raise up the oppressed, to rejoice with the happy. The very recognition of the source in this way by the subject involves the distinguishing and identification of self by the subject, at least in relation to the particular call, as having some food to share in face of the hungry, as professionally equipped to help in the case of doctor with patient, and as in a position to promote individual or group freedom in relation to those enslaved by economic or racial or other social discrimination.

The distinguishing of source and subject in the moral situation implies at a deeper level the recognition of the source as a different world, the world of the other precisely as other. This may not always or often form an explicit part of moral awareness but it is implicit in the dynamism of the distinguishing act itself and available to reflection at any stage. To distinguish and recognise the other as other in this more profound, if frequently implicit way introduces one to an awareness of a world which overlaps and shares some common area with one's own (otherwise the basis for distinction would be missing), but whose creative centre of understanding and meaning, order and relationship is always finally distinct from one's own, from oneself. To recognise the other as this other in the more precise way possible through the particular moral situation is to distinguish other and self more fully, to have a fuller awareness of self as different, as this particular self. The other-recognition which occurs in the moral situation (and every human situation has a moral dimension, is a moral situation in a definite sense) involves equally a fuller recognition or identification of the self as this precise self. The growth in self-understanding, in identification of the self, depends on this interchange with others in which the others (groups or individuals) are recognised as fully as possible.

The fuller implications of this discovery and identification of the self through the recognition of the other as other cannot exhaustively be treated here. Such recognition and identification occur in some degree, however slight, in every situation. The relationship of self to other (in our terms of subject to source of moral call) provides the basis and the dynamism for the discovery/awareness of the diverse aspects of the self, for self-identification or the integration of these diverse aspects into the understanding of the self already achieved. There is considerable variation in the use of many of these terms and in the description and interpretation of the experiences involved here. There are non-personal, sub-personal, as well as personal realities confronting the subject. Does this understanding of himself also derive from his recognition and understanding of these non-personal realities, whether stones or trees or animals, phenomena of nature such as landscapes or sunsets, earthquakes or landslides, fresh air or cancerous cells, the products of human creativity and industry, Shakespeare's *Hamlet* or the Beatles' 'Yellow Submarine', the RB 211 or river pollution? The human and moral subject finds himself in some relationship to these phenomena. This discovery and understanding of them and his relationship to them depends on the language, thought and experience categories of the group into which he is born. It depends on the human others. His distinguishing of non-personal realities and of himself in relation to them includes some reference to the personal realities of the human others from whom he has been born and with whom he has developed. His knowledge of non-personal realities is based on his sharing a common world of words and concepts and experiences with his fellow-men. It follows on admission to their world. In so far as it contributes to his understanding of himself it derives from his sharing of their understanding (but it does not necessarily remain at or coincide with this). It derives from a certain understanding of people. Information about the world in which the subject lives becomes a means to self-understanding as it becomes a means to other-understanding. The world of self as a personally-centred world emerges and is understood in relation to other personally-centred worlds. The sub-personal constituents of the personally-centred world of any subject are discovered and identified in relation to another personal pole.

In so far as they enter into the constitution and self-understanding of the subject as subject they are never merely sub-personal. Physiologically a smile may be no more than a twist of the lips, a fold of the skin based on certain muscular contractions. Personally it is much more, as a genuine or false human communication with the other, pleasurable recognition of him or pretence. It expresses the movement of recognition and acceptance in particular situations. As both a natural and a learned response, based on man's physiological and psychological capacity but learned in community as an expression of pleasure at the other, it provides a simple illustration of how sub-personal cosmic realities enter into the constitution of the worlds of self and other and acquire a moral dimension through reference to these personal poles. This applies to the resources of nature such as food and fuel as well as to its catastrophes like floods or earthquakes. Beyond the most elementary data of the cosmos itself, the human development or distortion (e.g. ecological) of its resources give them an obviously human frame of reference and integrate them into the human worlds of the poles of moral encounter. So direct personal confrontation with the sub-personal can lead to self-understanding in so far as it reflects a deeper confrontation with the wider personal world.

Otherwise information about the non-personal world may promote technology in industry (including the Ph.D. industry in the so-called humanities) but it does not enlarge self-understanding. Many of the limitations of modern education and accompanying social organisation may be traced to this 'information syndrome'. This is perhaps another way of saying that one's relationships with non-personal realities are human and so have a moral aspect in so far as they are relationships with other personal realities. And the call to recognition of the other in the moral situation (the human situation taken morally) may be to recognise the source of their moral significance in personal realities.

The non-personal realities are properly distinguished from and related to the world of self in so far as personal others enable one to distinguish that self as a personal world. Without personal others or recognition of them the non-personal in so far as they could be distinguished would be just extensions of the self, constituents of its world in varying degrees. This might involve the danger of reducing the personal self to non-personal and result in various kinds of depersonalisation or alienation (separation of the person from its true self). In so far as there is preoccupation with things rather than persons, with information *about* rather than personal recognition *of* (as in certain anthropological and sociological studies, for all the necessity and value of such information in a subordinate role), with techniques and technology rather than personal expression and creativity, this danger is very real. The situation in which we live can thereby be depersonalised, dehumanised, demoralised. One of the major tasks of the present is undoubtedly to awaken and develop the personal dimension in a technological world. It is a primary moral call, a moral call to extend moral sensitivity, to allow the moral dimension of our situation to emerge.

This digression may help to underline and explain the essential first stage in the moral response, the emergence of the moral subject as subject-in-response-to-source and his discovery and identification of himself as subject, as a particular personal world, through distinguishing and recognising the source as a particular but different personal world. The other-recognition and self-identification go to the core of both personal-source and personal-subject but along a line defined by the particular situation. In the medical situation doctor and patient are in a professional relationship which nevertheless involves them at their personal centres. In the political situation the members of the body-politic, the citizens in their various political capacities may meet as voters or representatives but the meeting goes to the personal centre of each one. So the morality of political encounters, for all the conventions and conventional language, is decided according to the same criteria as other encounters, and parliamentary privilege or diplomatic language, whatever their value otherwise, may not be used to slander or deceive.

The encounter of subject and source at their personal centre, along the line defined by the situation, determines the recognition and identification necessary and possible. The subject recognises the other as other but under a particular aspect. The self-awareness awakened is awareness of the self as self, a world in communion with but radically distinct and different from the other under the aspect defined by the situation and the call expressed in the presence of the other. Just as one discovers that one speaks with an Irish accent when listening to English people or American or even that one is Irish in relation to various foreigners, English, French, or other, so in the continuum of one's life-situations one becomes aware of what constitutes the world of self when confronted with the gift and call of the world of the other. The child gradually learns to distinguish his mother and so himself as a personal centre. This is a continuing task which expands as he encounters more people inside and outside the family. It is a life-task as he only gradually through these encounters gets to know who he is.

Phase Two: Other-respect and Self-acceptance

The recognition of the other in the situation with the accompanying recognition of the self is a part of a single dynamic movement of which the next stage is respect for the other as other. The call to recognise the other as an independent given (gift) world implies a call to respect this independent other world in itself. This recognition includes or implies respect for the other as this different world. To subordinate this personal world to oneself, to use it as one uses an object, is to fail to recognise its true character and fail to respect it. Respect for the other in his difference and acceptance of the other in his independence have rebound effects or implications for the respecting and accepting of the world of self. Other-acceptance and other-respect involve self-acceptance and self-respect. There is continuous interchange between the two aspects of this single movement and as one grows in other-acceptance and other-respect one grows in self-acceptance and self-respect.

It may be useful to pursue the investigation of this phase a little further. It is of course just one phase in the overall interchange between subject and source, and not one completely distinguishable from the phases of recognition or response. All three constitute a single dynamic movement in which it is, hopefully, enlightening to distinguish those three phases. As they are not completely distinguishable and distinct, so they do not occur in a strict time sequence suggested by the order presented here. This order is primarily psychological and has a certain human logic about it. It may in many instances correspond to a chronological order. But human interchanges are not regular, tidy phenomena which may be readily analysed. The three phases mentioned here can be verified in such interchanges but they will overlap and recur and be combined in different ways and with differing emphases. So the fuller recognition or respect may occur only after the response has been completed. Yet they are both at least implicitly present in the response itself. And indeed they may never become explicit in the subject's consciousness at all as he responds to the call of the other.

Respect is a qualification and further development of the notion of recognition. To recognise the world of the other as gift in its achievement and potential—for the sake of simplifying the discussion I ignore the threat element for the moment—carries a built-in call to respect the world in its difference, uniqueness, freedom. This respect lies along the same line as recognition but qualifies it or makes it more precise by accepting the independent worth of that which is recognised. Recognition of value, of the other person (or group), characterises the respect-phase. And as respect in this sense is a development of other-recognition, self-identity undergoes a similar development. Recognition and acceptance of the value of others enables one to recognise and accept the value of the self. Self-acceptance and self-respect will be as real and effective as one's other-acceptance and other-respect.

This may appear paradoxical, as the more conventional approach has been to regard self-acceptance and self-respect as necessary preludes to other-acceptance and other-respect. It is frequently maintained that one who is unable to accept others in their achievements and failures (in the husband-wife situation, for example, or even in the professional colleagues situation) has never accepted himself in his true worth and real limitations. It is, I believe, true that one who has not accepted self in this way cannot accept others. And it would be very hard to establish chronologically, even in a particular case, which came first. In line with my previous approach to the analysis of the moral phenomenon and human interchange as it occurs now, I do not propose to get involved in the history of anybody's psychological development. Other-acceptance and self-respect, like other-recognition and self-identity, are not primarily distinguished and separate in time. They may occur in varying order. The relationship is a dialectical one and the overall development is contemporaneous. At any particular time the person will be self-accepting to the degree that he is other-accepting and vice versa. What is important is to realise that the summons originates outside the self in the other. The call to respect the other is in that sense primary and the source of self-respect.

Other-respect and self-acceptance emerge as call and are achieved along a particular line defined by the situation of encounter between subject and source. In the verbal communication situation, which must be further defined in various ways—as preacher with congregation or teacher with pupils or parent with small child, plus the further possible refinements of their generic situation—the call to respect the other involves speaking audibly in a language known to the listener with some awareness of the listener's world of ideas and interests and needs. It means avoiding personal abuse, manipulation of the person through flattery or threat, manipulation of the truth to enhance one's own argument, manipulation of the situation to increase one's own power or prestige. Respect for the other in verbal communication implies far greater concern for the truth and makes far greater demands on the source than the simple prohibition of lying as always wrong in itself (and then modified by the complexities of mental reservation) or the manly call to speak the truth come what may.

In the critical attitude to 'authorities' which is sometimes mistakenly described as a 'crisis of authority' the lack of respect for the intelligence and integrity of others (however unintentional) prevalent in the statements by authorities (civil and ecclesiastical) plays an important role. Not that the lack of respect operates one-way. Sycophantic currying of favour with the authorities by echoing and endorsing their every word and refusing to communicate in a mature and critical way is no less lack of respect for the people in authority and for oneself. And so is contemptuous rejection of them and of all they say. Respect like recognition is a two-way process. Everybody has the call. Somebody has to start in each particular situation. Leaders, through office or ability, if they are to act as leaders in a human community must do so first of all in their respect for the world of the others.

In the individual's situation the respect is called for and manifested along a particular line. I have tried to illustrate this by taking the line of verbal communication. I might have taken the line of sexual communication and tried to show how respect for the sexuality of others was a permanent call and that the response to that call involved the acceptance of one's own sexuality. The various swings through which sexual *mores* pass from puritanism to permissiveness illustrate how far recognition of and respect for people in their sexuality may vary and be ignored or distorted. And today's vastly increased biological, psychological and sociological information on the whole question of human sexuality may prove a threat rather than a gift, if it is not integrated into personal recognition and respect. A permissiveness that trivialises sexual communication must inevitably trivialise people and diminish their respect for others and for themselves. While the interchange is sexual, the deeper reference is, as always, to the personal centres. A puritanism that tries to repress sex as dirty must degrade the people also, while a romanticism that ignores its earthly roots will be equally distorting.

At the group level the call to respect is no less urgent although frequently much more difficult to define. A group is not centred in the same way as a person. It has not the centre of consciousness and self-consciousness or of decision which a person has. Members may leave the group or they may belong to different and even conflicting groups. Nowadays everybody belongs to a series of overlapping groups, more or less structured and organised, with some of them in quite sharp conflict. Not all these conflicts will be clear-cut as that which a Catholic Unionist or Protestant Republican experiences in Northern Ireland, although some will be sharper still and such conflicts exist for everybody in some degree.

Despite this diffusion and confusion which the group exhibits as a subject or source of moral call, it is clear, as I said earlier, that many of our most pressing moral calls originate from groups, from oppressed and deprived groups almost everywhere : Northern Ireland, South Africa, South America,

North America and so round the world. On a world scale these obviously deprived groups form a formidable part of the human race. Response to them in any appropriate way is beyond the range of individual activity. It must be a group-response, requiring group-awareness of the others and their call, group-respect for them and finally group-response involving group-decision. One may not then evade the group as moral-subject and yet pretend to deal with moral call as it is experienced today.

What pattern of awareness (recognition) may or should be displayed by any particular group as subject in relation to the other (individual or group) as source of moral call, it is very difficult to say. The mass media of communication so triumphantly developed in recent time can and do play an important role. But they are media, not disembodied and omniscient authorities. They need to be critically used and placed in a context of the group seeking to enlarge and make more precise its recognition of other groups in their otherness. Recognition clearly involves respect for the otherness of the other source-group. It may not be so clear how this respect is essential to the subject-group's acceptance of itself. Unlike the individual a group may appear to recognise and accept itself without any reference to others. There are difficulties here which are not precisely the province of the moral analyst, although he can scarcely evade them.

Isolated groups may exist and certainly have existed in a way that suggests that the self-identity and self-acceptance of groups is not correlated with their recognition of and respect for other groups. Even for such isolated groups my earlier analysis may still hold. If the group does not identify and accept itself in relation to some outside group it has to identify itself in relation to sub-groups or at least individuals within itself. This would certainly provide one kind of group identity and acceptance, and create situations of moral significance for the group as group. Tribal laws in ancient Israel or ancient Ireland and others much antecedent to those groups must have originated in this way. Of course until it actually becomes aware of other groups, apart from itself, the isolated group cannot identify and accept itself as this *distinctive* world—that is, distinct from other similar worlds or groups. It may, however, achieve a certain identity in relation to the world beyond the group by its attitude to the non-human world which it knows, the physical world of the cosmos or a superhuman world in which it believes, the divine world of the god(s). These two, the cosmic and the divine, may be closely intertwined for many peoples but they do help to give a setting and so a certain sense of identity to the isolated group. The setting and identity mentioned here are not the kind I normally have in mind here when speaking of a group's identifying and accepting itself through the recognition and acceptance of others. Yet as I mentioned earlier, this trans- (sub- and super-) human setting provides a wider and necessary context for the human (and so moral) interchange between individuals and groups.

The isolation of some groups in the past or even in the present does not invalidate the point I wish to make about recognition and respect, identity and acceptance. There is, however, another possible objection. The moral call, which, according to the criterion accepted earlier, should issue in deeper and fuller communication between individuals and groups, would appear to depend on the recognition of sameness not of difference. The call for food and freedom for blacks in South Africa or North America stressed the fact that they are human like the whites. The stress in Northern Ireland is on the need for Catholics and Protestants to sink their differences and accept their common status as Ulstermen or Irishmen. This objection has already been answered in principle at an earlier stage of analysing the moral dimension of human interchange. Without some common framework, no interchange can take place. Recognition of the other as other is only possible within the framework which, however undeveloped, allows for mutual recognition. The fuller communion will develop this framework but in a way which will enable the individuals or groups to be more fully themselves, more developed in their difference and so mutually more enriching.

At the individual level this may be easily enough seen, and the role played by respect for the other and by self-acceptance in the fuller communion, yet deeper differentiation, scarcely requires any further illustration. For groups this respect and this acceptance are considerably more complex and elusive and the combination of communion and differentiation almost defies description if it is verified at all.

Recent history of the group problems I have mentioned does offer some insight. In the early history of black-white relations in the U.S. the opponents of slavery and later of various kinds of exploitation and deprivation appealed very properly and emphatically to the fact that those exploited and deprived were human beings and American citizens just like the more privileged whites. In varying ways culminating in the great Civil Rights Movement in the 1960s the effort of white and black leaders alike was based on 'sameness', 'just like us'. At a later stage (although there were earlier prophetic voices like that of James Baldwin) many black Americans no longer accepted this white American identity imposed on them and wished to define and identify themselves at least partly in terms of their African origins and not exclusively in terms of their American context. Black Power is one, if an extreme, manifestation of this. This development may be the immediate source of confrontation and conflict, but if mutual recognition and respect by the groups black and white develops properly it could lead to an enrichment of the whole community of the U.S. by the fuller communion which embodies deeper differentiation rather than a more comfortable adjustment of the Negroes to the American (white) way of life and the final acceptance of them in this by the whites.

A similar and parallel development may be observed in Northern Ireland. The confrontation of Protestant and Unionist with Catholic and Nationalist provided little relief for the deprived Catholics or indeed in other ways for the predominant or, as they saw it, besieged Protestant over fifty years.

E

Harmony seemed possible only through the acceptance of Unionism by the Republicans or of Republicanism by the Unionists, and these appeared impossible demands. The Civil Rights Movement broke the deadlock and for a while it appeared as if some Catholics and some Protestants could unite on a basis and a programme that transcended the old divisions. This did not last very long however. And at the time of writing the groups are in as bitter a confrontation as they have ever been. The Civil Rights appeal to a common humanity or common Ulster or Irish heritage, even to common British standards of justice and fair play, has to a large extent been buried by the actual violence in the streets and the rejection by political leaders on each side of the basis for negotiation proposed by the other. At this stage recognition of, acceptance of and respect for differences may have to go a good deal further than any constitutional guarantees for the Republicans and Catholics in a reformed Northern Ireland parliament or for the Unionists and Protestants in a new federal Union of the Republic of Ireland. Any satisfactory solution must take account, in a way which past proposals did not, of the deeper differentiation of the two groups historically and racially as well as politically and religiously. It must enable them through mutual recognition and respect to be fully themselves within a unity that does not automatically make one master and threaten the other. At any rate it is failure in the past to recognise and respect the other group which is now being paid for in the streets of Belfast and Derry.

The attention to differentiation as a source of mutual enrichment in these two instances illustrates the respect of other to which the group no less than the individual is summoned. If the analysis proposed here is correct, other-respect by the group as moral subject should involve self-acceptance. Despite the threat to self-respect apparent in respect by whites for blacks as blacks in the United States, respect by Northern Ireland Parliament and Unionists for Catholics and Republicans as such, with its social and political consequences, it is only such respect that will gradually eliminate the insecurity and lack of self-acceptance which the present uneasy, if not downright violent, interchange indicates. It is only when a group has properly valued the Republican as Republican or the black as black that it can feel any genuine security in its own Unionism or whiteness. For the individual and the group other-respect is the correlative of self-acceptance.

Phase Three: Other-response and Self-development

The third phase in the subject's reaction to the source in the moral interchange is what I have called the response. Again it is important to emphasise that the three phases form a dynamic unity in which one or other phase may be predominant but in which the other two are at least implied. So it may happen that recognition is all, that no further moral response is necessary or possible. Jesus' look at Peter as recorded in the gospel accounts of the Passion is a dramatic example of an interchange in which recognition was all. In less dramatic circumstances a look or letter of acknowledgment can mean a lot to somebody ignored or insecure or lonely. The recognition should include respect and constitutes the appropriate response but it is simply recognition. In other situations a spontaneous—perhaps anonymous—action of help does not pause for recognition or respect but certainly presupposes them. To hark back for a moment to the original structure of the situation, the presence of the other as gift implies a thanksgiving-awareness as suffusing every possible response and emphasises endless combinations and variations of the three phases in the subject-source exchange.

The response itself in this framework is the subject's effort to meet the immediate need of the source as manifested in the moral call experienced by the subject. It can obviously take innumerable different forms from a reassuring smile of recognition to laying down one's life for the other. And it operates at group as well as individual level.

In striving to meet the need of the other as source of call, the subject has to summon whatever resources are available to him and are appropriate to the call. If he himself has no appropriate resources available, his call becomes a call to find someone who has. A person without any medical skill who comes on somebody seriously injured in an accident should try to find as soon as possible somebody who has this skill. In so far as he has resources, immediate or mediate, the subject should try to organise and actualise them in service of the other. In this service of the other resources at different levels may be needed, physical resources to lift somebody who is seriously ill, psychological resources to reassure him, intellectual and educational resources to help him medically, material resources like hot water and bandages and drugs and surgical instruments. In organising and actualising (making actual) these resources in the service of the other, the subject is also organising and actualising (bringing into action) himself. In the response to the call of the other, he is polarised or unified in a particular way; he has to recognise and utilise the resources that are his; by his action he brings into being not only service of the other but through that and in pursuit of that he brings into being a new feature of himself. Through this response he achieves or actualises more of himself. He creates a further aspect of himself. Other-response is self-developing or self-creative.

There may not be any immediately perceptible evidence of this in a particular situation. It cannot be empirically measured in the way one would measure muscular development. Yet if there is a genuine personal response from the subject and not a kind of computer service by remote impersonal control, some fresh actualisation of the subject takes place and he changes, however minutely. Such a change will be an expansion of his world or, to change the image, a further creation, if in fact his response has been to the other as other in his need. It will be a contraction of his world, if the response has been self-centred, endeavouring to use the other and his need for the self. In this instance there will be no breaking out of the self but an attempt to draw the other in, with the contracting dynamism which that involves.

That such responses vary considerably in the demands made

on the subject and the service given to the source hardly needs elaboration. The variation derives from the needs of the source, their kind and intensity, as well as from the resources of the subject and his willingness to use them. And two further important qualifications of the subject-in-response are relevant at this point. One has already been stressed earlier in dealing with the recognition-and-respect phase : the response, however specialised its channel and however slight its intensity, involves at least minimally the subject at the centre of his being, if it is personal and moral action at all. Of special importance to this phase is the second qualification of the subject as being in exchange with and called to respond to a number of others, while his resources at any particular time for any particular case are limited and in some cases may not be appropriate for action at all.

This is a most important qualifier at this third phase—the limitation of the resources of any person or group and the indefinite range of demand that may be made upon them. While one may not refuse recognition or respect to another, it is a fact of life that one may have to refuse further more concrete response because the only resources available are already 'bespoke'. Such a refusal in such circumstances does not make recognition and respect a sham. The limitation, however, could easily be made an excuse for inactivity in the face of serious need or for discrimination in favour of already privileged people. Much of the political failure in which we share takes one of these forms.

To ensure that there is neither inactivity nor discrimination, it is necessary for the subject (individual or group) to establish a list of priorities in regard to different needs and various sources of moral call. This list will vary from subject to subject and from time to time for the same subject. And it will frequently have to be departed from as a plan of response in face of unforeseen and emergency needs. For his list of priorities the subject (individual or group) will naturally consider those for whom he has particular responsibility as husband or parent or teacher or politician or citizen, but openness to the wider world for which the individual or group also has responsibility will demand that the basic needs of the wider group will not be sacrificed to the less urgent if real needs of those for whom one feels more immediately responsible. Here one immediately encounters the very thorny question of social justice within a particular state (two houses or cars for some, no house or flat for others) and between states (can there ever be adequate assistance to the starving unless some countries are prepared to take a cut in their standard of living? What hope is there of even 'Christian' politicians endorsing this, if, for example, Irish politicians are unwilling to ask for one per cent of the people's income for overseas aid?). At any rate there must be a list of priorities if the resources are to be used and used fairly for the real needs. That list has to be fairly flexible and its range should be deliberately indefinite.

In discussing the limitation of resources, the subject may well be tempted to settle for the status quo, to allow the apparent lack to become an excuse for inactivity when his call is not only to use but perhaps to create the resources. A commonplace excuse of this kind in education, the Church, and the wider society is that 'the pupils or teachers or people or bishops would not be willing to do it', that 'they do not see it like that', that 'it is not politically possible'. Morality like politics is an art of the possible but some things can be and should be made possible. It is in the creation of resources for response in face of the seemingly impossible that the highest moral achievements occur. Such were the achievements of Mahatma Gandhi and Martin Luther King in the political and social fields. It does not always require the genius and dedication of a Gandhi or King. If people were more alert to the call to creativity and to its possibilities in all kinds of situations, they would not so despairingly or, more commonly, so smugly say that unfortunately there is nothing to be done. Before anybody says that, he should have examined his own failure to find the resources and see how far it is the case that he is unwilling to take the trouble of finding or inventing the necessary resources. The self-creativity which is dependent on other-respect passes through a deeper stage of development where the resources have to be found or invented as well as used.

Disintegration and Reintegration

The other-response and correlative self-development or creation occur in the human interchange of the moral situation. In transcending self to recognise, respect and serve the other, the self as subject reaches the other as other in these different phases. This self-transcendence to reach the other as other involves a certain disintegration of the world of the self including its previous settled relationship to the other. The break-up of the previous synthesis or bond or communion is called for by the other in his present need. (If this is very slight the disturbance or break-up will be correspondingly slight.) The recognition of the other as other in this new stage, respect for him, and response to him, amount in varying degrees to a certain disintegration of the subject and his relationship to the other. But this should then issue in a reintegration of subject and relationship at a deeper level of *communion* achieved through the reaching out in recognition, respect and response, and at a deeper level of *differentiation*, achieved for the subject in a fuller self-identification, self-acceptance and self-creation. In the ideal situation the interchange is mutual and the differentiation and communion are achieved by both. In the actual situation the interchange may be much less than mutual and the reintegration, differentiation and communion for the subject, for example, may not in a particular case be at all in proportion to the energy expended. This will not deter him from further response because, while it is completed in mutual exchange, it does not seek this but is concentrated on the other in his need. One of the difficulties which any human analysis of morality as it is experienced must deal with, is this lack of the reciprocity which moral experience seems to demand but which it has often to do without. This is so often the case that it becomes almost a test of true moral activity 'that there was nothing in it for me', not even acceptance or gratitude.

The disintegration and reintegration, which the true moral response to some degree involves, occurs over the total range of moral calls and activities. And it affects the moral subject at centre. Whatever the particular area of interchange, medical care or commerce, politics or sex, the subject who truly recognises, respects and responds to the other as source is modified at centre by this activity. As already indicated, the modification, which I have suggested takes the form of disintegration and reintegration, may vary enormously in depth and intensity. It may be very slight, or it may involve the subject radically, profoundly altering him by shattering his previous world of the self and its relationships to others, or it may occur anywhere along this spectrum.

In seeking for a turning point along this spectrum, the moral analyst refers back to his criteria for distinguishing good and bad responses, good and bad relationships, good and bad moral states. If the response is predominantly other-centred, if the relationship is predominantly other-centred, if the person is predominantly other-centred, one applies the label good. To be predominantly self-centred is on these criteria bad. Clearly a critical response is that which turns some relationship or somebody from being predominantly other-centred or self-centred into its opposite. Such critical actions may occur in any area of activity but their critical character is measured by their conversion-capacity for this particular subject from self-centred to other-centred or vice versa.

The Critical Response and Basic Direction

A separate chapter would be needed to explore fully the implication of this approach to the 'critical' response. A few points may be underlined here. Its critical character derives from its conversion-ability. The response must be capable of changing the subject's basic direction—towards the other or towards self. Responses of such significance, however, which are in line with the subject's basic direction confirm this direction in a serious way and have an important role in the subject's remaining in it. Critical responses may be other-centred or self-centred, good or bad. Although their frequency cannot be established *a priori*, the significance attached to them and their ability to change the subject's basic direction suggest that they may be relatively rare. At least they are unlikely to be daily occurrences, unless the subject is as change-able as a weathercock. As they can be good or bad and as the ability to change the subject operates in both directions, ease of change in one direction would appear to be balanced by ease of change in the other. Sub-critical responses lack this ability to change the subject. They may express and deepen the subject's basic direction (as other-centred or self-centred) or they may frustrate and evade it. If of themselves they cannot change it, they play a role in strengthening it against change or in preparing it for change. This role will vary with the intensity and frequency with which they involve the subject.

In this discussion two other aspects have figured, one explicitly and the other implicitly. Explicitly I have mentioned a number of times the subject's basic direction and qualified this as self-centred or other-centred. This was a natural follow-on from the reference to criteria distinguishing good and bad responses, relationships, people. Where they are predominantly other-centred, they are good. The predominance refers back to the ambiguous character of the structure of the moral relation-ship, combining gift-embodying-call with threat-provoking-fear and the consequent ambiguous character of the response and of the subject-in-response. In face of this ambiguity, pre-dominance not exclusiveness in other-centredness or self-centredness is what one may expect. Basic direction, however, applies to the subject and to the response. The subject is in response to all kinds of sources in all kinds of ways. That is how one recognises his basic direction. But one is not talking about the predominant character of a particular response, slight or critical, but of a (more or less) permanent set or dis-position of the subject himself. This settled disposition is revealed (to himself and others) in the untidy mass of his interests and responses but it is first of all brought into being by these responses and in turn brings further responses into being. A man's basic direction at any particular point in his history is the fruit of that history and a powerful influence in the future course of his life. It is not of course finally decisive at any point in history. It can be changed. That is the function of the critical response. But all this involves some discussion of an aspect which has been mainly implicit up to this, time and history.

The subject's basic orientation is the fruit of his historical responses, his responses over a time which together have been predominantly in one direction in such a way and to such a degree that the subject has acquired this kind of settled disposition. In the development of disposition or basic direction time plays a key-role. It would be impossible to trace the ebb and flow of the awareness and response to others which after a certain period sets the subject predominantly and stably in one direction. It may take quite a long time for some people. It presupposes a certain centring of the person, his unification and polarisation to the degree that one can speak of him as a whole as having one moral direction. This of course may be changed and will certainly be disturbed later. Its first emergence, however, is an important element in his moral development and might be described as first moral maturity.

I am not interested here in the discussion about the first moral act, which to me is a quite different problem and depends a great deal on how one defines morality and moral activity. Despite the very useful work done by Piaget and his successors on the emergence of moral consciousness they do not seem to consider how far their moral philosophical presuppositions determine the framework of their investigation and so of their results. The illuminating ideas of the super-ego developed by psycho-analysis, supposing that they are well-authenticated by empirical observation, might not be as conclusive in reducing all early childhood activity to the pre-moral if the concept of moral derived from some recognition of others as others rather than simply from rules or values. The philosophical discussion about the first moral act also depends on one's concept of morality, which can only be derived from adult experience, and to some extent from empirical observation of children, which can be notoriously difficult to interpret especially for philosophers!

First moral maturity is a different concept, although it is of course no easier to accept or to verify. I invoke it as a subordinate feature in my discussion of the basic moral direction of the subject, to draw attention to the historical element in this basic direction and in its first appearance. It does, moreover, allow one to speak of moral maturity in varying degrees and prevent the confusion of the moral maturity appropriate to a teenager with that appropriate to an adult.

I should like to distinguish this basic moral direction or orientation (perhaps a better expression) from the fundamental moral option discussed by many moral writers today. In so far as I understand the matter, both expressions coincide in their understanding of the present attitude or direction of the moral subject. The influence of the fundamental moral option on future action seems very like what I suggested for the basic orientation. Change in either would presumably involve the same kind of critical action. I am less happy about the accounts of how this fundamental option comes into being. The expression itself suggests some grand dramatic choice and the literature generally does not seem to do justice to the gradual, historical, mainly implicit formation of the basic orientation which my experience suggests. This may be a matter not only of experience but of categories of thought and of cultural difference. Again the change in basic orientation will be through a critical response but one which is prepared for in time, in history. The critical action is the culmination of a process which may not be adverted to until the critical action itself occurs. Again the 'fundamental option' language suggests some more dramatic manifestation of what is certainly a profound change.

The relation of the fundamental option to the final option at death which some Christian writers discuss is not the province of the strictly moral analyst. The fate of the basic orientation, however, does present him with another puzzle, which must be taken up in a later chapter.

I have carried on this discussion largely in terms of subject-in-response-to-source where that source is seen predominantly as gift. To complete this picture it would be necessary to go over it again with the same attention to the source as threat. I do not think that it would alter our understanding of the various phases of recognition, respect and response. Where the challenge to let gift predominate over threat was not accepted by the subject, he would fail in true recognition, respect and response. He would turn towards the self and, if this were a critical response and he had already been other-centred, he would become predominantly self-centred. This disintegration would lead to a lower level of self-identity, self-acceptance and self-development. His basic direction would be self-centred and evil. Should he accept the challenge but fail to find reciprocation in the source, he would in some sense have achieved greater identity, acceptance and development but with the continuing wound of incompletion and rejection. In the actual experience of some people at least, this is a not uncommon feature. To be true to experience one must record these failures and the pain they imply, the pain also involved in any serious moral response with its accompanying disintegration and the final disintegration which that response may require in laying down one's historical existence for the other. All this the moral analyst observes, analyses and, in acceptance of the pain and the death, applauds. They are part of the way of life of the moral subject. Their undoubtedly puzzling features transcend the limits of his observation and analysis and will be dealt with in a later chapter.

4

Morality and Jesus Christ

MORALITY has been analysed as a human phenomenon and in isolation from the analyst's Christian faith. It is the task of this chapter to examine that analysis in the light of Christian faith, to see how far that faith may illuminate the human experience of morality, how far it coheres with it, how far it may be possible to establish some intrinsic connection between living faith and moral experience.

Historically a close relationship between religion and morality in life and in reflection is readily verified. Within the Jewish-Christian tradition such a close relationship has always existed. As I suggested at the outset moral theology or Christian ethics has taken this relationship for granted and sought to derive a system of morality from the religious events and teaching recounted in the tradition. The validity of this procedure is not in question here. A different approach has been adopted, beginning not with 'revelation' as embodied in this tradition but with personal moral experience and so a fresh attempt must be made to relate morality and Christian belief.

Questions Raised by Moral Analysis

Although some of these questions are raised later (in chapter 10, 'Discerning God's Action in the World') it will be useful to begin by indicating how the analysis of morality tends to take the analyst beyond the bounds of strictly moral discourse into questions of fundamental philosophy of life. It is at this level naturally that the relationship between Christian faith as the basic philosophy of life of this particular analyst and moral analysis finds its obvious starting-point.

The interrelation between moral subjects (whether human individuals or human groups) which lies at the basis of the moral experience has been described in gift-threat terms where the moral obligation or call was understood as call to enable the gift to triumph over the threat. The gift of the other (and of the self), recognised, respected and responded to, should characterise the acceptable moral interchange. A good moral response is an expression of thanksgiving. It is at least possible to ask whether this attitude of thanksgiving has any final justification; whether the thanks terminate with the human other(s) with whom the moral subject is confronted; whether the gift of the other(s) does not raise a question about the giver.

More searchingly, a question arises about the unconditional character of the moral call and the associated inviolability of the other as gift. In some moral situations certainly and especially, in my view, the supremely moral ones, the unconditionality of the call is manifest so that one feels bound by it, whatever personal disinclination or disadvantage may be involved. The unconditionality which appears at least in the recognition and respect due to the other as a different and inviolable world which one may not use, possess or eliminate, and to which one is admitted by invitation only, inevitably demands some explanation. Why are unconditionality and inviolability applicable to human beings in this kind of analysis and not to other cosmic realities? The answer is not to be found in further moral analysis but in the transmoral sphere of *Weltanschauung* or fundamental belief about the nature of man and the world.

In recognising and responding to the world of the other, the moral subject reaches a world beyond the self, transcends the self. This self-transcendence, expressing the openness of the self to others, occurs in varying degrees in reaction to various others during the history of the particular moral subject. It is a possibility which never seems more than partially fulfilled. The possibility frequently breeds an aspiration for completion which no single other or range of others can satisfy. The moral experience reveals a capacity and an aspiration which it does not seem able of itself to meet or finally justify. It simply places a question-mark.

The openness and reaching out of the moral subject takes place in time. It requires time for its development in the subject's continuing life and in his concrete situation. With that temporal or historical background it may be said that the moral experience is always directed towards the future. The moral response moves from the present into the future, however immediate that future may be. In a rather different sense we are here concerned morally about the future at present. Efforts to promote world peace and development are at least partly inspired by concern for generations yet unborn. This concern is explicitly articulated in current preoccupation with pollution and destruction of the earth's natural resources. Concern then for future generations which do not in any cosmic sense yet exist, is a respectable and effective moral concern. It is also a puzzling one for the moralist. As a moral analyst he will record it. His attempts to justify it will go beyond his moral analysis. He has encountered another puzzle at the limits of his analysis.

Attention has so far been centred on the positive and gift aspect of the other in moral experience. Earlier analysis indicated that the other also appeared as threat. The negative dimension of the moral experience has its own puzzles or question-marks. The threat which we pose to one another, individually and collectively, affects in different ways every aspect of our lives in the family, at work, in our local, national and international communities, even in religious communities and the Church. The triumph of threat over gift is expressed in failure to respond to the other as other; in rejection of response by the other; in the intractability of certain situations, between husband and wife for example, or between races or creeds or classes as exemplified in hostility and war around the world.

The questions are many. What final explanation does one give to the existence, extensiveness and strength of this threat element? (With a satisfying cosmic explanation one would expect to eliminate it entirely by personal and social 'engineering'.) How does one justify continuing attempts to make the gift triumph over the threat by renewed attempts at response in spite of failure or rejection or intractability? How does one explain the human phenomenon of hope? What kind of sense does one make of the actual triumph of gift over threat, of reconciliation and forgiveness and communion? The moral analyst who is also, hopefully, a human being cannot filter out such questions. They arise naturally in the course of his reflections although his immediate task and expertise does not offer any answers.

The unconditional demand to respond to the other which the moral subject experiences is rendered very questionable by the historic fate of the other in death. How can one justify such unconditionality and inviolability in face of the eventual reduction of the person to disintegrated matter? Death threatens with absurdity the whole moral enterprise. This is emphasised by the common and to me acceptable recognition of the heroic moral value of laying down one's life for the other in extreme need. How does it make sense to treat as the highest moral activity the end of all further moral activity in empty death for the sake of somebody who is only temporarily removed from the same empty fate?

The particular questions posed here arise out of the structure of morality as revealed in the earlier analysis. Those questions, that analysis, are not the only ones possible. They are verified in the experience of this particular analyst and hopefully are recognisable to some of my readers. It should be possible on the basis of quite a different experience and structural outline to encounter somewhat similar limit questions, which the moral analyst cannot finally avoid but which he cannot answer on the basis of his moral analysis itself. What has been described here in terms of recognition, respect and response to the other, as characteristic of the moral experience and determinative of moral good, might be summarised in terms of the 'problems' of human freedom, goodness and love. These are age-old problems. It may be no harm to draw attention to them as problems for human understanding and justification in a context in which they can be advanced as data of experience and in the awareness that the problem of evil and hatred distresses many people who are not sufficiently alert to the fact that the existence of goodness and love, even intermittently, also creates serious problems of adequate explanation. One may not obscure the problem of evil by the problem of good but one can at least balance it.

The purpose of this discussion is not to use the moral experience and its attendant problems to prove anything about Christianity. It is rather to open the moral discussion to other levels of discussion so that the Christian and theologian can find points of connection. The moral experience has its own coherence and consistency and has to be respected fully for itself and not just used as a stepping stone to something else. Yet it is not closed from other areas of experience and their analysis whether social, psychological and physical, or religious and ultimate. The openness at the level of religious or ultimate philosophy of life is expressed here in the questions which have just been raised. The task of the Christian theologian in confronting his moral experience and analysis with his Christian faith involves discussing how far these two aspects of his personal and intellectual life connect intrinsically, how far they are at least coherent and compatible with one another, how far they illuminate one another and how far his Christian world view responds to the kind of ultimate questions which the moral experience suggests.

Christianity is not the only world-view which might be invoked to confront the moral experience as presented here. Much might be gained by some comparative study of world-views in relation to this or similar moral analyses. However, in accordance with the method of this essay I shall confine myself

F

to the Christian world-view because it is my own. Even if I had the time and space to discuss others, I could not do so at the same level, since I do not accept them. It will be necessary of course to indicate from time to time where other views might be relevant at least in showing why one accepts Christianity instead.

Living Faith in Jesus Christ

As a Christian theologian confronting his own moral experience I take as my theological base an acceptance of or faith in Jesus Christ which is personal to me but born of and dependent on the wider Christian community to which I belong. The Jesus Christ whom I accept as key to understanding human existence, its origin and fulfilment, I recognise as living and accessible to me now in the community of his disciples. His presence to me in and through this community is signified and more precisely focused in the basically constitutive and distinguishing elements of the community, word and sacrament.

The personal faith of the theologian which is the springboard of his theological reflection is both a community reality and a historical one. Jesus Christ is encountered in the historical community of the Church. The understanding of man and the world which he offers to me I can discover and more fully explore in this community and the tradition which forms it. Such exploration can be and is pursued in many different ways. Selection is partly determined by the theological task in hand and partly by the personal equation of the theologian. Fidelity to the community and its tradition excludes selectivity and bias so that the selection must be related to the fullness of that tradition in its relevance to the particular task, and the personal equation operates only in the theologian's attempt to understand all that relevant fullness.

Acceptance of Jesus Christ and so of the God of Jesus Christ as the ultimate reality confronts the believer with a tradition older than Jesus himself or the community of his disciples. Correct understanding of Jesus' role and significance, of Jesus'

God, demands attention to the earlier tradition into which he was born and within which he was formed and which he both confirmed and transcended. The manifestation of God which took place in Jesus cannot therefore be understood without attention to Jewish tradition. Our understanding of the present and of Jesus' significance for it must be in continuous dialogue with the past. Yet that significance is even more clearly related to the future. Christians are not people preoccupied with the past. That past helps us to understand the present but the present itself is moving into the future and not simply the historical future of tomorrow or next year or next century, important as that is. There is a definitive future on which Christianity hinges as it has been made known in the risen Christ. Fidelity to the past, concern with the present and openness to the future have their own particular significance for Christians.

Structure of the God-man Relationship in Jesus Christ

Within the all-embracing purview of Christianity, cosmic, historical and social, Jesus Christ is the centre and climax. He forms the critical link between, on the one hand, cosmos, human history and society, and on the other, their ultimate source, significance and destiny which the earlier Jewish tradition called Yahweh and Jesus described as God his Father. The God-man/cosmos relationship may be well described in all its various phases and dimensions in the accepted biblical word, covenant. The historical phases of the covenant are basically the Mosaic or Old Testament (covenant) and the New realised in Jesus Christ. However, the preparatory phases of the Mosaic covenant, particularly that with Abraham constitute important elements in the Israelist and subsequent Christian understanding of total historical relationship between God and mankind/cosmos.

The different dimensions of the covenant may be discerned at least embryonically at the different stages but emerge more clearly at one or other. The origin of man/cosmos from the God of Israel receives its most explicit treatment in the creation stories but it remains a recurring theme throughout the historical development of the covenants and re-emerges in the person and teaching of Jesus Christ as presented in the books of the New Testament. Here it is absorbed into the predominant themes of the New Testament: the incarnation or Jesus' sonship of the Father, the salvation/redemption/liberation of man and the cosmos from sin and evil, the fulfilment/consummation of man/cosmos in the resurrection as already accomplished in the risen Christ. In the Old Testament, salvation and liberation provide characteristic and predominant themes, and in terms of the recovery of the divine goodness originally manifested in creation but disrupted and obscured by man's sin. God's continuing involvement with man is directed towards overcoming human failure and consequent division between man and God, man and man, man and cosmos. Rejecting the ultimate origin of his existence and significance, man's alienation affects his relations with his fellow-man and the cosmos in which he lives. The divine involvement reached its climax in Jesus Christ, fully human and cosmic, and at the same time the incarnate Son of God. In him sin, division and alienation have been finally overcome and man has been restored to himself, his world and his God.

The individual believer and theologian enters consciously into this divine achievement as it was accomplished in Jesus Christ, and prepared in the Old Testament. In reflecting on it this particular theologian is struck by the insistence in the tradition on the divine initiative at all stages of the relationship between God and man/cosmos. Cosmos and man come into existence through the originating activity of God. Personal relations are established and renewed, in spite of man's failure, by the continuance of the divine initiative. The climax of all this in Jesus Christ entirely transcends the power, the demands, even the expectations, of man. Man is not presented as passive recipient. He is expected and indeed summoned to respond personally to the divine initiative in his religious, personal and social life. In the personal relationship which the divine initiative is seeking to establish or restore, personal response on man's part is essential.

Gift and Call

The Judaeo-Christian tradition can be seen to have a basically gift-call structure. Divine revelation is increasingly understood in terms of God's gift of himself to his people. His people form the *qahal*, assembly of the called, who on the basis of this divine gift are to behave as his people. Creation including man is the first of God's gifts and embodies a call to man to respect and develop it. In the further development the creation-gift is taken up into the more personal giving and relating known as revelation, to which man is called to respond. So the divine gift embraces in this world-view all that is available to man as actually or potentially enriching. In particular it embraces man himself and his fellow-man as gift involving call. The creation stories, the covenants with Noah, Abraham and Moses, manifest the same gift-call structure. The Decalogue spells out the call which the divine self-giving to Israel as his people involves, not only in terms of response to Yahweh but also in terms of response to one's fellow-man. Response to God and to neighbour, with at least the implication that they come to one as divine gift, summarises the lifestyle of the Old Testament. When the divine giving comes to full term in Christ, the gift aspect of one's fellow-man reveals him as brother of the incarnate Son and adopted son of the Father, sharing in the very divinity itself. For the man who answers the call of Jesus, living is a matter of loving, loving God and one's fellow-man. To respond to the least of men is to respond to Christ himself. That is the measure of the gift of each man and of the awesome responsibility of the call implied. In the achievement of Jesus, however, the very gift includes the capacity to fulfil the awesome responsibility. God is working through him to enable all men to reach perfection. Salvation means that the divine initiative is sufficient for men to recognise, accept and live by the gift, in other words, to answer the call.

Threat and Fear

In the chequered pattern of Judaeo-Christian history, failure
and division and even destruction seem to play as large a role
as loving divine initiative or loving human response. God's gift
of himself and of his human and cosmic creatures does not
inevitably meet with a loving response. The history becomes
a history of salvation because it is also a history of sin and evil.
In this context the creative and loving God takes on the
character of a God of fear. His creatures, in particular mankind, experience him as threatening them with punishment and
actually inflicting that punishment. The divine self-giving
becomes, in the context of man's failure to respond, threat to
man. The created gifts of the same God, gifts both human and
cosmic, share in the division and alienation and assume the
same threatening character in relation to one another. The
divine promises and activity are directed towards overcoming
the division and threat and towards restoring the original gift-
and-communion-in-gift relationships.

In endeavouring to understand my own Christian belief by
entering more fully into the history of the community in which
I found and maintain it, I am increasingly struck by the gift-
threat correlation as exemplified in the biblical accounts of
that history. The misleading and now entirely outmoded
description of the God of the Old Testament as a God of fear
in contrast to the God of the New as a God of love had its
origins in the emphasis on the punishment or threat of punishment attributed to God for man's failure to respond to his
loving initiatives. It was always in the context of man's failure
despite God's loving care. More deeply it might be understood
as the transformation by man of ultimate reality as gift into
threat by ignoring or distorting it. Reality, and above all
ultimate reality, will continue to exist and assert itself whether
man recognises and responds to it correctly or not. Where
he fails to do so its enriching possibilities for him will be
excluded, he will be in conflict with his own deepest reality,
threatened by it and perhaps finally destroyed if he does

not manage to return to the reality which he has rejected.

Israel's understanding of the origins of the world and man as recorded in the Book of Genesis, provides a remarkable insight into how reality in its ultimate fullness as well as in its immediate human and cosmic expressions can be primarily gift and yet emerge as threat through man's failure to recognise and respect and respond to it. I find in the changed pattern of relationship between the Creator and his creatures, between the human creatures themselves, and between these and the cosmos, a means of understanding the ambiguities and failures in my own life and in the life about me. The creation story itself, in the two versions in chapters one and two, is entirely a gift story. All that is, comes from God. The supreme gift is man himself, created in the image of God, called to enjoy his special friendship and entrusted with the rest of the creation as special gift and charge. The sexual duality of mankind is related in chapter one to the image of God in man. In chapter two the mutual love and unity of husband and wife is underlined in the divine search for a companion fit for man, the story of woman being created from the side of man and the ecstatic acceptance of her as his wife by the man. Adam's love-song and the writer's comment on their acceptance of their nakedness confirm this. The two stories are therefore completely dominated by loving giving and receiving. Gift is paramount.

Chapter three at once highlights the call which all this divine gift involved for man and man's failure to answer that call. The temptation was a suggestion as to how man might usurp God's place, make himself the ultimate reality. His ecstatically accepted partner is cast in the role of primarily yielding to the temptation and then leading him to destruction. Gift and threat are already changing places. The sense of threat is further manifest in the couple's awareness of their nakedness and of the need to cover it. The gift of sexual duality from now on bears the stamp of threat. The ultimate threat is experienced by them as they become aware of the presence of God and attempt to hide themselves from him. In the subsequent account of their punishment, the cosmos itself in its resistance to man and the cosmic forces within themselves as exemplified in child-bearing, take on the same threatening character. The extent of the threat which man poses for his fellow-man is most fully revealed in the Cain and Abel story in chapter four, where the threat issues in fratricide, the destruction and murder of one's own brother. It is possible to follow the story of threat qualifying if not entirely replacing gift right through the Old Testament. All the covenant stories reveal gift and threat elements. The warnings of the prophets call attention to the threat implicit in failure to recognise one true God of Israel in worship and in life.

The history of Israel is seen as a whole in terms of the divine initiative and gift being frustrated and thereby turned into threat by Israel's failure to respond, a failure frequently described in terms of its seeking after false gods. The idolatry of substituting some religious idol or some human passion or power or money or pleasure (which the idol may also represent) for Yahweh as the one true God is the characteristic failure of the people of Israel. It remains a type of all human failure. It is the perfect recipe for conflict at the deepest level of reality, for the predominance in human life of threat over gift.

For all the human failure, the continuing divine love expressed in achievement and promise, and finding genuine if qualified response from the people of Israel, enables one to enter into the Old Testament as a history of faith and hope and love. The threat and the fear cannot be denied or ignored but do not finally obscure the gift. The God of the Old Testament is a loving and giving God. And it is the promise of definitive gift and love, of liberation from the threat and driving out of the fear which sustains the people of Israel as above all a people of hope.

Jesus Christ as Gift and Threat

When the hope of Israel is eventually fulfilled in the definitive gift and love embodied in Jesus Christ it would be quite mistaken to think that the definitive gift did not contain its own elements of threat. If the God of the Old Testament cannot be characterised as a God of fear to the exclusion of love, the God of the New cannot be characterised as a God of love to the exclusion of fear. In a very important sense because the gift has reached its climax so has the threat. Because 'from him to whom much is given much will be required' (*Luke* 12 : 48), the very fullness of the gift has enormously extended the risks of refusal, increased the extent of the threat.

The words of Simeon in Luke's gospel (2 : 34) that 'this child is set for the fall and rising of many in Israel' touch on a theme that recurs in the sayings and events recorded in the books of the New Testament. John in his prologue describes how 'the true light which enlightens every man was coming into the world. He was in the world and the world was made through him, yet the world knew him not. He came to his own home, and his own people received him not. But to all who received him who believed in his name he gave power to become children of God' (*John* 1 : 9-12). As the stakes were so much higher, the threat of failure became much more fearful. Tyre and Sidon would be judged less harshly than the towns of Chorazin and Bethsaida because of the mighty works done by Jesus in them (*Luke* 10 : 13 f.). The Queen of the South and the men of Nineveh would condemn Jesus' own generation because that generation had been confronted by somebody so much greater than Solomon or Jonah (*Luke* 11 : 29-33). Denial of Jesus before men entailed denial by Jesus before his Father (*Matt.* 10 : 32; *Luke* 9 : 26; 12 : 9). The gift of God that was in Jesus' reconciling men with the Father and with one another (2 *Cor.* 5 : 18-20; *Gal.* 3 : 28) would be also a sword of division, setting a man against his father and a daughter against her mother (*Matt.* 10 : 34; *Luke* 12 : 51-53). The gift which exceeded all threat (*Rom.* 5 : 20), embodying the love which drove out all fear (1 *John* 4 : 18), became for his own people a threat of such proportions that they sought to destroy him and in the immediate historical sense succeeded. The rejection of

Jesus to the point of killing him finally established the extent to which the people to whom he came experienced him as threat rather than gift. Subsequent history has confirmed, within as well as without the fold of his explicit disciples, how human weakness and malice can transform the ultimate gift into the ultimate threat. The God of Jesus Christ is undoubtedly and supremely God of love. Our failure to recognise and respond to that, our substitution of our own supreme loves and ultimate realities will result in collision with the truly ultimate and finally break us.

Coherence between Moral Analysis and Christian Belief

Perhaps I have adequately shown, in a personal but not artificial way I hope, how acceptance of Jesus Christ as basic to a world-view coheres with my analysis of moral experience at least in broad outline. The gift-call/threat-fear dimensions of moral experience which seemed to me one justifiable way of structuring the moral relationships in which I found myself, reappear at a different level of reality in attempting to present the basic structure of my Christian belief in its historical and social genesis. It might be objected that the coherence is too neat and depends on my prior acceptance of Christianity. Of course it is not possible for me to divorce myself from my previous history and education, or from my present basic Christian stance. The same impossibility applies equally to the non-Christian moral analyst. However, it is possible I believe, as I maintained earlier, to follow the moral experience as one finds it without confusing it with the religious or world-view. It is not so easy, perhaps not possible, to separate out the cultural structures of one's moral experience. Again this applies equally to the non-Christian. One is always carrying on this activity within certain cultural categories. To recognise this is to begin to allow for it and to enable one to be open to moral analysts from quite different cultural backgrounds. The point here, however, is not the cultural one but that of religious or basic philosophy of life.

It is my contention that the moral experience can be

adequately distinguished from the religious, in order to per-form the kind of analysis I have attempted. The validity of that analysis must be examined for itself. If it is found to be valid at least as one way of presenting the reality in a certain cultural setting, loosely described as that of the West, that is sufficient for my purpose. In the same way I cannot claim to have offered more than one line of understanding through the rich strand of Christian faith and the Judaeo-Christian history in which it is born. If it is a valid line that again suffices for me. If both my analyses have validity I should expect to find some people accepting my moral analysis without being willing to accept my theological analysis (and this might apply to Christians as well as non-Christians), or accepting the theology without the moral analysis.

It is possible to pursue the coherence and even convergence between Christian faith and moral experience beyond the broad outlines already indicated. One of the points neglected in so much moral analysis and emphasised if not adequately followed up in my own is that of the community aspect of morality in terms of the community or group acting as moral subject.

It is difficult to exaggerate the stress on the corporate subject of response in faith within the Judaeo-Christian tradi-tion. In the Old Testament this might appear to be stressed almost to the point of undermining individual personal re-sponse. It is the people, Yahweh's people, which is always at the centre. Outstanding individuals, such as Abraham or Moses, kings or prophets, are defined in relation to the people. Israel as the people is the true recipient of God's gifts and the proper subject of the call which these gifts embody. Yet the individual is never entirely submerged in the corporate body. Personal self-awareness and individual responsibility emerge in contexts as distinct as those of the demands of the Decalogue and the spiritual wrestlings of Job.

In the New Testament there is undoubtedly a greater emphasis on and deeper understanding of the individual person his dignity and responsibility (gift and call) as disciple, brother, adopted son. Yet the corporate identity is not obscured. It finds a different modality for the New Israel in the identification of his disciples with Christ as branches of the vine (*John* 15), members of his body (1 *Cor.* 12), living in Christ, sharing his life, sonship, very divinity. The community of believers has in Christ a unity of life and activity which does not on the one hand devalue or diminish the individual believer as human person and adopted son of God or on the other hand deny the relationship between Christ and all men. He is the new Adam. In him the divine initiative has finally prevailed for mankind. All men belong to the redeemed human race of which he is the head. In the day-to-day exchanges whatever is done to any, even the least of men, is done to him (*Matt.* 10:42; 25:40). The unity of mankind, established in him in principle and manifest in the body of believers, is part of the divine gift to mankind which embodies a historical call to which all men must respond and for which they are empowered in Christ. The group as subject and source of moral call finds a new significance and universal extension in the understanding of mankind deriving from Christian faith.

The moments of recognition, respect and response in the moral experience are readily paralleled in the religious or faith experience of the Christian. A more interesting question is how far elements such as integration and basic orientation as we have used them in discussing the moral experience have any correlates at the deeper Christian level.

Integration and Disintegration

In world-view terms personal integration might be interpreted to mean unity at man's deepest level: acceptance of his ultimate origin and meaning, dignity and destiny. For the Christian it means acceptance of his creation in the image of God and consequent dependence on him but also the recognition that the gift of human existence is now to be understood in terms of sonship of the Father manifest and made available in Jesus Christ. The integration as gift and call has transcosmic significance. The bestowal of divine sonship involves a call to be 'perfect [or integral] as your heavenly Father is perfect' (*Matt.* 5 : 48), and to share the maturity of Christ (*Eph.* 4 : 13). Such a level of integration is primarily gift and is adequately described only in terms of a new level of existence : for this a man must be born again (*John* 3 : 8), made alive again in Christ (*Eph.* 2 : 5), 'created in Christ Jesus for good works' (*Eph.* 2 : 10), a new creation therefore (2 *Cor.* 5 : 17) putting on the new man (*Eph.* 4 : 22-4).

It is integration with the Father in Christ that provides the basic orientation of faith, hope and charity which finds expression in man's work. It is what comes from the heart of man that matters (*Mark* 7 : 1-23; cf. *Is.* 29 : 13). The good tree bears good fruit and the evil tree, evil fruit (*Luke* 6 : 43f). Bearing good fruit depends on abiding in the vine who is Christ (*John* 15 : 4). Existence and persistence in the life offered in Christ reconciles man at his most profound (2 *Cor.* 5 : 18-20). This reconciled and integrated man is impelled to do the works of the Spirit of God who has been poured forth in his heart (*Rom.* 8), the works of sons of the Father and brothers of one another, works summarised by Jesus himself as love of God and love of neighbour (*Mark* 12 : 28-34), where neighbour includes everybody, even one's enemies (*Matt.* 5 : 43-8). The basic Christian orientation is God-centred and neighbour-centred and these two are different sides of the same coin, as the New Testament so often makes clear (cf. *Rom.* 13 : 8; *Gal.* 5 : 14).

In the concrete situation of human failure and self-centredness profound change of heart is demanded of the individual. The call to repentance or conversion provides the opening theme of Jesus' own preaching (*Mark* 1 : 15 par.) and is continuously repeated in the first preaching of his disciples (*Mark* 6 : 12; *Acts* 2 : 38; *passim*). A change of the most profound kind is expected, expressed as new birth, and it is expected to be the source of a new life-style. Christian conversion creates then the new basic orientation. Repentance and conversion clearly involve disintegration of the old world, destruction of 'the old self' in Paul's words (*Rom.* 6 : 6). In all this the emphasis is on the saving work of Christ, his delivery of mankind from the bonds of sin. The world which has to be disintegrated is the self-centred world of sin. The radical character of that disintegration finds its most appropriate expression in 'death and resurrection'. For Jesus 'unless a grain of wheat falls into the earth and dies, it remains alone, but if it dies, it bears much fruit' (*John* 12 : 24).

'Whoever would save his life will lose it; and whoever loses his life for my sake and the gospel's will save it' (*Mark* 8 : 35 par.). The true disciple must be able to drink of the cup which Jesus drinks (*Mark* 10 : 35-40). The rebirth of baptism is understood by Paul in a similar way : 'We are buried therefore with him by baptism into death, so that as Christ was raised from the dead by the glory of the Father, we too might walk in newness of life' (*Rom.* 6 : 4).

The dying to self and living to God and the neighbour in Christ involves pain and suffering for which the Christian must be prepared, to the point of taking up his cross daily to follow Christ (*Mark* 8 : 34 par.). Yet in the refreshing presence of Christ the burden is indeed light (*Matt.* 11 : 28-30). The blessings which are to characterise his followers issue in joy and fulfilment even in this world (*Matt.* 6 : 25-33). And of course the sufferings which may now have to be endured cannot be compared with the glory yet to be revealed (*Rom.* 8 : 18).

Repentance or conversion is not the end but the beginning. The summons to walk in newness of life demands continuing growth after the fashion of the seed sown on good soil (*Mark* 4 : 3-20). The call is to the perfection of the Father (*Matt.* 5 : 48) and only he who perseveres to the end will be saved (*Matt.* 10 : 22)—that is, will achieve final fulfilment or integration on the pattern of the fulfilment of Jesus. It is the efforts of the good soldier of Jesus Christ or of the good athlete or farmer (2 *Tim.* 2 : 1-6) that lead to 'the crown of righteousness' which the author of the letter believes the Lord has in store for all who love him (2 *Tim.* 4 : 8). In that struggle and growth new stages of development will involve movement and change

of a disintegration and reintegration kind until the final disintegration of historical death is reached, to issue in the final
reintegration of resurrection, anticipated for us and guaranteed
to us in the death and resurrection of Jesus Christ (1 *Cor.* 15).

For all the radical transformation achieved by rebirth or
conversion and the 'superabundant gift' (*Rom.* 5), on which it
is based, the new life remains threatened by the old forces of
sin and evil. The insistence on the need for perseverance (*Matt.*
24:13 *et al.*), the danger of putting one's hand to the plough
and then looking back, the warning that Christians carry their
treasure in earthen vessels (2 *Cor.* 4:7) indicate some of the
reminders, in the New Testament writings themselves, of the
possibilities of relapse into one's former sinful state. Judas's
betrayal of Jesus, Peter's denial of him, the desertion of the
other disciples, the attempted fraud of Ananias and Sapphira
(*Acts* 5:1-11), the divisions at Corinth (1 *Cor.* 1:10-13), the
immorality of the man living with his father's wife (1 *Cor.*
5:1-2), provide concrete instances during Jesus' own life and
in its immediate aftermath of a disintegration of the Christian
in his new existence. As the community of Christian believers
grew, the threat and reality of such failure multiplied also.
The Christian Church had always to reckon with cockle among
the wheat (*Matt.* 13:24-30; 37-43); the individual Christian
found himself permanently at risk and sometimes, whether in
face of persecution or out of personal greed or selfishness, he
proved a bad risk. Sin as disintegration of the life of love was
not simply banished by the achievements of God in Jesus
Christ. The grace to bear with the temptation was always
available and where that was not availed of the further grace
of a fresh repentance and conversion was known to be at hand.
What Tertullian called the second plank of salvation, the post-
baptismal reconciliation of the sinner in the rite of penance
was seen as one of Jesus' particular gifts to his Church in com-
missioning it to extend his saving work to all men and bring
them the forgiveness of their sins. In a manner which could not
be discerned or anticipated in moral analysis, the common
experience of failure and of the need to have it forgiven and

overcome, finds internal meaning and external expression in the Christian sacrament of penance.

Possibility of Intrinsic Connection

Coherence between the structure of my moral experience and that of my religious experience as a Christian believer, which I am satisfied I have discerned in analysing my own life at these two levels, may remain entirely unconvincing to the outsider. Even for me it might be a formal and extrinsic coherence with no intrinsic connections bearing either life or light from one to the other. It is necessary to explore the possibilities of any such connections as a support or corrective for myself and perhaps as a further illumination for the reader.

The obvious way into this exploration is to consider the puzzles which the earlier analysis of morality presented and which demanded that the analyst go beyond his purely moral analysis. The question marks discovered at the limits of that analysis left the way open for further discussion of a more intrinsic connection between morality and world-view, in my case Christianity.

The first question arose out of the gift aspect of the moral situation, the call to give thanks which it naturally implied and the puzzle about the source of the gift or ultimate giver, if such could be envisaged. Without entering into the complexities which follow from even the formulation of such a question as that of gift (in the context of moral analysis) pointing to some 'giver', and without claiming to establish any conclusive argument from gift to giver, I do feel justified in calling attention to the possible illumination which a moral analysis which recognises gift and gratitude might receive from a basic Christian understanding of the world. The world of creation and salvation as manifest in Christ is gift, gift from the Father, ultimate origin and destiny. The basic Christian attitude is one of gratitude, as we see in the very name for its central ritual, the realisation of its deepest mystery and achievement, eucharist. The Christian eucharistic stance confirms, illuminates and for the individual Christian connects with the human moral response to the gift dimension of the other in each moral situation. If the highest moral response is mutual celebration of the presence of the other as gift, the Christian can fully endorse the primacy of such a celebration ethic.

Another question, more challenging because it takes one more nearly to the roots and limits of moral experience, is the unconditionality of the moral call and the correlative inviolability of the person or human other. I find it hard to accept any purely intra-cosmic world-view as accounting satisfactorily for these aspects of the moral experience. To explain the unconditionality and inviolability in the context of the highest conjunction of molecules we know does not appear very convincing to me. What is the criterion of highest? The Christian doctrine of the distinctive creation of man in the image of God, his further call to friendship with and even to sonship of God, the ultimate reality, at least confronts one with an account of the origins and meaning of man which confirms the unconditionality and inviolability recorded in the moral analysis. The sense of otherness which played such a large role in the earlier discussion arose from a view of the other as a different world, a mystery to which one could be admitted by invitation. The Israelite conception of Yahweh as the holy one highlighted this mysterious element and in words (holy, holiness) which basically meant other, totally other. Created in the divine image, man has from the beginning shared in this otherness or holiness of God. The Christian can thus discern a truly intrinsic connection between his moral experience and the final mystery of reality whom he addresses as the God of Abraham and Isaac, of Moses and the prophets, the God and Father of his Lord, Jesus Christ.

The possibility of and aspiration to self-transcendence which the analysis of moral experience reveals may of course be doomed to final frustration. Certainly it is hard to see it being finally satisfied in historical experiences with cosmic beings. In the Christian perspective it reflects at the moral level the ultimate openness of man to the fullness of reality as it is available to him from God in Jesus Christ. Without confusing

G

the two levels of reacting or discoursing it may still be possible
to discern a justifiable movement from the one to the other.
For many Christians today, including myself, the self-transcendence of the moral responses and the encounter with the
human other which it involves, may well be a very effective
gateway to genuine religious experience or at least to some
confirmation and understanding of the final mystery.

The puzzle about moral obligations to generations yet unborn might of course be re-interpreted as some kind of cosmic
imperative. But if they are genuine personal obligations and
we are to be held accountable for wastage of energy resources
or polluting the atmosphere by people who have no kind of
existence just now, there remains a certain puzzle. In a theistic
and particularly in a Christian framework our accountability
to God as Father of the generations to come and equally
concerned for their welfare as for ours, offers a certain
justification. In the more precise and dynamic vision of Christ
as the head of creation and all men and the final point to
which mankind and the cosmos is reaching out, those who
make up the present generation of Christians are called to
promote development of the whole world towards its final
completion, conscious that they should hand on the cosmos
which has been entrusted to them to future generations in a
more developed—not a more decayed—state. The Christian's
concern for the future is for the gifts which he has been given
and which he must respect as they are intended by the divine
giver for all men, to whom the Christian is bound to remain
open in love and with whom he hopes to enjoy the final
consummation.

The problem of personal failure and man's need for forgiveness has already been discussed. It may be argued that not all
men experience this need. My point is rather that some men
do, at least this analyst does. To a genuinely felt need,
Christianity offers a manner of coping which has undoubtedly
been abused as a magical erasure of past failures and a licence
for those of the future, or as an inducement to a kind of moral
paralysis in those who allow themselves to become preoccupied

with past failure. All Christian institutions in common with all human realities operate as gift and threat. Properly understood and exercised Christian repentance and forgiveness help to reintegrate individuals and communities fragmented by failure and rejection. They explicate and deepen what a strictly moral analysis may discover but does not finally explain.

To go on trying despite failure or rejection or apparently insurmountable difficulties inherent in the situation seems an important part of the human moral enterprise, although not at all easy to justify. Hope which forms the spring-board of such effort requires at least explanation if not justification. The Christian finds both in the person and achievement of Jesus Christ. In his death and resurrection, failure and rejection at their ultimate were confronted, accepted and in the transforming power of God revealed as finally overcome. The absurdity which threatened all moral endeavour through the emptiness of death has also been overcome for the Christian in Jesus' own triumph over death. Moral activity reaches its completion according to Christian understanding beyond human history in the reintegration of the resurrection.

Centrality of the Person and Achievement of Jesus Christ

Coherence, illumination and at least a degree of intrinsic connection exist, it can be maintained, between moral experience and Christian faith. The link, however, is not primarily to be found in teachings or writings but in persons, and above all in the person of Jesus Christ. Considered within its own limits, Christianity turns on the person and achievement of Jesus Christ. So does its significance for morality. The more basic Christian approach therefore to morality is not by way of the explicit moral teaching of the Bible, important as this is, or even by way of the explicit moral teaching of Jesus or his first disciples as recorded in the New Testament. The central reality for the Christian theologian reflecting on the moral experience is Jesus himself in his personal existence, mission and achievement.

In his personal existence, Jesus constituted the centre-point as well as the end-point of the relationship between God and man which was founded in creation and is destined to be completed in the Parousia. As the Word of God made flesh, his very existence marked the ultimate in the divine self-giving to man and the world. In his human acceptance of his mission he responded to the divine initiative out of the genuineness and fullness of his humanity, in all his human activity, culminating in his human dying to his Father at the hands of man for men. The divine endorsement of his responses unto death by the transformation of the resurrection, proclaimed to his disciples, and through them to the world, the profound meaning and permanent value of all that is truly human, including the moral dimension of human existence. It is at this level of the final significance (meaning and value) of moral living that Jesus Christ most effectively relates to any analysis of human morality. That significance is of course filled out in the present analysis by coherence in structure, basically gift-call qualified by threat; by illumination of the human other-ness with its unconditionality of call and inviolability of person by offering some ultimate satisfaction to the process of self-transcendence involved in moral response; by providing some grounds for continuing to hope in face of continuing failure; by enabling one to understand death as a way to fulfilment rather than an emptiness which would throw the validity of the whole moral enterprise into doubt.

Qualities of Christian Response

The moral interchange between individuals and groups presents the Christian with others whose worlds immediately reflect the ultimate and absolute reality he calls God and Father. His recognition, respect and response must in turn reflect this awareness, an awareness demanding expression in the quality of his whole responsive attitude which should be characterised in the first place by an attention and sensitivity bordering on the worshipful or awesome. One is in the presence of the absolute mystery, the ultimate reality. I do not suggest that great formality is required in a casual situation. Formality can often be cold and insensitive, far from expressing any awareness of mystery or deeper reality. Neither is there question of spending time in focusing one's attention on the dignity and mystery of each particular individual or group.

The meaning and sense of otherness which Christian moral understanding and living imply could have serious implications for the deepening of one's religious and prayer life. The inadequacy of their prayer which many Christians today confess, has many diverse and tangled roots. One of these roots may be a certain loss of awareness of the richness and mysteriousness of human day-to-day living, of human relationships, of human moral demands and responses. Such an apparently prosaic experience as asking and receiving the time of day from a total stranger whom one will never meet again, with all the implications of how two moving pieces of earth whose paths momentarily coincide should have reached such a sophisticated level of communication that they know what they are talking about, that they live in a world so organised that time of day is meaningful and shared, that one should have the initiative to ask a total stranger and the other the ability and willingness to respond truthfully, could provide the starting-point for an intense awareness of the mysterious reality of the cosmic and the human without which an awareness of the ultimate reality of the divine may be crippled and even artificial and empty. A genuine moral sense of the human other should nourish the Christian's sense of the divine other. It is this kind of enrichment which many people's prayer needs. In the person and activity of Jesus Christ the connection between the divine and human other had an intensity and continuity which continually challenges us in our moral and prayer lives.

A further important characteristic of the Christian response to a moral situation is urgency. Those who are unwilling to make such a response too easily use respectful attention to all petitions to escape their real obligations. (Pilate remains the classic case. Too many Christians in situations of gross social immorality follow his example.)

The urgency imposed by Christian awareness in the moral situation derives from the fuller understanding of the dignity and mystery of the human other as image and son of God. In very many situations this awareness has overtones of urgency in time. Dilatoriness is frequently employed as protection from both the risks of response and the guilt-feelings of refusal. So many personal and social needs are subjected to delaying tactics by people with the power to do something but who resort to time-wasting rationalisations instead. The time factor is included in a wider sense of the word intended here. For the Christian, the other as gift and call presses or urges more sharply because of the revealed identity of this other in Christ. The demand penetrates more deeply and precisely as a demand of a brother in Christ. The failure to respond has more serious implications as rejections of Christ and of his Father (*Matt.* 25). The reality of the call and of response or failure involves one with ultimate reality.

To give flesh and blood to the characteristics of Christian response one must return to the gospels. Without getting enmeshed in all the complexities of contemporary critical exegesis, it is possible to derive instruction and inspiration from the gospel accounts of how Jesus responded to different people in many different situations. His attention to the immediate physical needs of the people, his particular care for the poor and the ill, the spontaneity and warmth of his response, his sensitivity to the person, are some of the obvious characteristics of his behaviour. And while attention to these needs played such an evidently large role in his life and must have consumed a great deal of his time and energy, he never allowed them to obscure the deeper meaning and purpose of his life. His awareness of people reflected his awareness of Yahweh and his Father, and this was the dynamic force in his attention to people's immediate human needs—which, however, were always seen as subordinate to their ultimate needs of salvation from sin and liberation into the kingdom of his Father.

The Moral Teaching of Jesus

Whether as mediator (connecting link), meaning or model, Jesus Christ in person and achievement remains the central role in the theologian's efforts to offer a Christian understanding of morality. Person and achievement were of course interpreted by him for his disciples. Their records include a good deal of explicit moral teaching which the theologian of morality has to consider. The fuller exposition of this teaching as it is recorded in the gospels is the continuing historical task of the total Christian community. Here it will be necessary and sufficient, I trust, to draw attention to basic outlines and characteristics in an effort to relate these to the analysis of the moral experience already presented.

The primacy of love of God and the neighbour (*Mark* 12:28-31 par.) is the dominant theme of all New Testament moral teaching. Jesus' presentation of it here emphasises the continuity with the Law of the Old Testament. There is, however, a noticeable development in the depth and extension of the love demanded even for one's enemies (*Matt.* 5:43-7), with the result that it is described as a new commandment (*John* 13:34). The newness is explicitly related to the example of Jesus' own love. His moral teaching is the articulation of his own life-style.

The implications of the love-life advocated by Jesus, apart from finding their most appropriate expression in his own life and death, are spelled out in various ways in the recorded teaching of the gospels. Foremost in these records of his moral teaching are the accounts of the Sermon on the Mount (Plain) in the gospels of Matthew and Luke. These admittedly 'editorial' collections of moral sayings originally delivered in differing contexts offer remarkable insight into the radical nature and extent of the moral life which Jesus expected of his followers.

In addition to his express and elaborate advocacy of love of enemies, Jesus in the same spirit of love deepens to the point of transformation several Old Testament moral demands condemning murder, adultery, divorce, oaths and revenge (*Matt.* 5:21-42).

Because of the age-old debate about how the Sermon on the Mount is to be interpreted, whether in terms of rigid laws or of counsels only, it is necessary to insist on the relevance and possibility of the Sermon's instructions for all Christians. But they must not be approached in a predominantly legal spirit which makes them either impossible burdens for all or irrelevant extras for the few. Where morality is understood as a growing response of love which continually transcends itself as it seeks to meet the real needs of the others, turning the other cheek or letting go one's only cloak can be seen to be possible and relevant in particular situations, while they are always illustrative of the depth of the love to which the Christian is summoned.

The illustrative aspect of much of the teaching of the Sermon corresponds to that other great source of Jesus' moral teaching, the parables. Perhaps the most powerful piece of moral teaching in the New Testament is the parable of the Good Samaritan, yet it is impossible to reduce it to legal terms. The overall thrust of the moral teaching of Jesus whether summed up in love of God and the neighbour or presented more fully and systematically in the Sermon on the Mount or elsewhere, or offered indirectly in the parables, defies legal expression. Not that a rather superficial love-morality in which any activity may be called good which is *felt* to be loving, does any more justice to the teaching of Jesus than the legalistic excesses of the past. The hard and frequently very precisely formulated demands enshrined in Jesus' teaching reveal the true meaning of love and transcend the preoccupations of 'legalists' and 'situationists'. The gift-call understanding of the moral situation and moral life with its recognition of, respect for and response to the other(s) describes in stages the basic love character of the moral demand and activity, for which no legal formulation could ever be adequate. The gift-threat ambiguity and the call to enable the gift to triumph over the threat finds much more concrete expression in Jesus' call to love one's enemies. The various radical demands illustrating love which are found in the teaching of Jesus are entirely consistent with the open-ended character of the moral call and the continuing self-transcendence to new levels of integration which emerged in moral analysis; there is no need to resort to the two-storey morality of precept and counsel.

Conclusion

In his person and achievement as well as in his teaching Jesus Christ offered to mankind an understanding of human life and behaviour that far exceeds any ethical analysis. Yet it is possible to recognise a definite coherence between that person, achievement and teaching and the human moral life. There is a certain mutual illumination and confirmation discernible at least to one Christian moral analyst. And the questions arising at the limits of moral analysis open up for the analyst the possibility of an intrinsic connection between his moral living and its analysis on the one hand and his basic world-view, his Christian faith, on the other.

PARTICULARS

5

The Church: A Learning Community

WE ARE used to thinking of the Church as a teaching group. We ask ourselves the question: 'What is the Church teaching now?' I want to change this approach a little and put forward a view of the Church as a learning group; I would suggest therefore that sometimes a more appropriate question is 'What is the Church learning now?' This might seem a kind of smart, semantic trick, but I believe it rests on a basic understanding of the Church as the people formed by God's word, by listening to God's word, the believers, the people who are called to know Jesus Christ. And this being called to know Jesus Christ is a lifelong task. It is not simply a lifelong task for particular individuals; it is an age-long task for the group we call the Church. Who or what group could claim to know, to understand Jesus Christ? We are in the process of understanding him; we are, if we are true to our vocation, learning about him. The Church is a group of people called to learn the meaning of Jesus Christ and through learning the meaning of Jesus Christ to understand the meaning of mankind, because it is in that particular man that the meaning of mankind was incarnate. What we are learning in the Church is Jesus Christ. There is nothing else that we have to know. But we are learning as a group, as a community, and learning is a process that goes on in various ways in collaboration with different people, in confrontation with different people and goes on over time. It is a social and historical process.

How do we learn? How do we learn, above all, about a person, about the person of Jesus Christ? We learn, I believe, by placing ourselves in the presence of that person, by surrendering to the reality of that person. There are many aspects to this placing oneself in the presence of Jesus Christ. In this learning about Jesus Christ, we share a great deal of the ordinary learning process. I want to advert to some aspects of it here as they refer to this learning group we call the Church.

We learn by being open to receive. Placing ourselves in the presence of another is, in a different image, listening to that other. It is a particularly appropriate image for the Church because we think of Jesus Christ as the Word, as the Word of God to us, and we listen to the Word. This is the first way in which the Church is a learning community, in listening to the Word of God and receiving it. Receiving it not in a passive sense, in the way a vessel receives water poured into it, but in the extraordinary, active, self-surrender that is part of the human process of learning and of understanding.

I remember, as a university student, having to move from what were Newtonian physics to Einsteinian physics. And I remember the pain, the shattering pain, of trying to come to grips with something like space-time continuum in the Einstein sense. This kind of painful surrender operates in every learning process. But when it comes to learning in the sense of understanding a person, of understanding that person who is the Word of God, the surrender is even more demanding. It is a mysterious process whereby we are at once passive, receiving, being impregnated as it were, and on the other hand active, selective, picking out and picking up the threads, the ideas, the realities of Jesus Christ.

There is another aspect to this receiving. In so far as we receive the Word of God, in so far as we grasp this truth that is Jesus, we are driven at the same time to communicate it. And in the very process of communicating, our understanding changes. We learn by communicating as well as by listening. The trivial example of the lady at the cocktail party who says :

'Well, how do I know what I think about the war in Vietnam until I say it?' has a point because it is in the process of communication that we find out what the listening-learning process really is. I do not want to draw a sharp distinction between the two. They are part of a continuing dynamism in one's life, and I know, from previous experience, that as a result of simply trying to communicate with you about this, I shall learn something. The learning process is involved in communication so that when we speak of the Church as a listening and learning group, we must realise that the listening and learning goes on in the communication, whether preaching in the pulpit, religion teaching or personal counselling.

In that kind of verbal communication, we are still in the process of learning. We have to pick our way carefully, respect and choose our words because they are words in which we are trying to express the Word. And as we express, I hope, we expand because we learn and we understand something further. But this listening, moving into communication, moves further. It goes into action as the third part of the same dynamic process. As we listen to the Word of God, as we communicate it, if we would not frustrate either of these, we must do it; we must '*do* the truth', in the Pauline phrase. We must put it into action in the service of Jesus Christ, in the neighbour. And in the action we learn further. Doing is in a way the climactic learning. It is in this experience of giving oneself in service that one arrives at the fuller understanding. So the 'ivory tower' student who listens does not know what he knows until he tries to communicate it, and the communicator does not know the significance of it until he tries to do it. And so the Church as a learning community is a community that is increasing its understanding of the Word of God through the listening, communicating and serving.

I have presented all of this as if Jesus Christ were someone we could summon from the vasty deep and study, to sit at his feet and listen to him as the disciples did. Jesus Christ, we believe, is risen and with us, but he is not accessible to us as other people are. When we are talking about the Church as a learning community, learning in the sense of increasing its understanding of Jesus Christ, we must consider more closely where we concentrate this learning activity. What is the immediate object on which we centre? In this we are helped in many ways by recent conciliar developments, by the Constitution on the Liturgy, for instance, which drew attention so forcibly to the threefold presence of Christ to us; his presence in what we call the inspired word, Scripture; his presence in the rite or sacraments; and his presence in the people in the community. So that if we would place ourselves in the presence of Jesus Christ, if we would be this kind of learning community, we would have to attend to this threefold presence.

There is his presence in the inspired word of God, in our prayerful reading of it and listening to it. By prayerful I mean personally sensitive to all the dimensions of it; not any kind of pious, holy feeling. We attend to it as it is in itself. Then we attend again to the presence in the sacraments, particularly in the celebration of the eucharist, the sacrament in which the risen Christ becomes risen and present for us. But I would like to draw attention here more especially to his presence in the people. As a learning community, we are a human community, endeavouring to understand what is finally a personal reality, what is finally, indeed, a human reality. We are trying to understand, in Karl Barth's phrase, the humanity of God. And it is in the presence of the other human person that we find this humanity of God, that we learn what Jesus Christ means. It is in attention to them, in listening to them, in communicating with them, in serving them that we become Christians, for we are only in the process of becoming Christians. We have been called to follow Christ, to learn from him, to learn him. This is our life task. It is in attention to the others that we begin to understand Jesus Christ.

But who are these others? It might appear from the Constitution on the Liturgy that they are the immediate congregation present. It would be foolish to overlook the immediate congregation in the search for more enriching and better human others, to overlook the people next door in the search for people to whom we might give fuller attention so that we might learn Jesus Christ more fully. They are an obvious presence of Christ to us. We know from the Constitution also that the Christian congregation is representative of the whole Church. This is something that is perhaps of great significance today because most of us are fairly selective about the people within the Church from whom we are willing to learn. Most of us have our own sects. But, if we would listen to and learn from the Christ who is present with us, we have to listen to and learn from all members of the Church. We cannot, therefore, indulge in a sectarianism which will rule out certain people classified as right or left, conservative or progressive. The Church is full of classified materials that somebody or other won't touch, and these are all human beings sharing the humanity of God. We must overcome this kind of sectarianism if we are to be a genuinely learning community. The sectarianism we talk about is not simply divisions within the Roman Catholic Church. The Christians who are separated from us, more formally, although often less basically than some Roman Catholics, are a presence of Christ to us to which we must attend and from which we have a great deal to learn in listening, communicating, and service. The waves of the learning Church spread out over all Christian bodies.

But if we are to think of the Christian Church as learning Jesus Christ in his presence in the world in word, in sacraments, in people, we have to advert to two important other lines. One is the historical line. If we are to learn Jesus Christ, we have to learn him through the various historical manifestations that reach back through the history of the Church to Christ himself, and then back into his Jewish and Hebrew origins. If we are to be attentive to God who manifested himself in Jesus Christ, then we must listen to these people. We must listen to the Christians of the nineteenth and the fifth as well as the twentieth century, or the first. There is, therefore, a need in our Church if it is to be a truly learning community to keep open lines of communication with the past. These lines of communication with the past are not simply for the sake of scholarship or archaeology but that we may understand the present.

We belong also to the future. If we are to attend to the presence of Jesus Christ, we have to attend to the future. We have to attend to the future in the conventional eschatological sense, the final consummation of the kingdom. There is a great significance in how we live our lives personally and communally as people directed towards the future, as people whose understanding of Jesus Christ is not of someone who can be grasped now, who is in that sense fully and totally present to us now, but of someone who is ahead of us, to whom we are coming, and importantly, also, to whom future generations are coming. So we have to keep our lines of communication open with the future generations as well as the past. We have to learn about Jesus Christ, learn Jesus Christ, from those who are now coming into existence as human beings, and we have a responsibility for those who are as yet unthought of. In our learning Jesus Christ we will be future-oriented in that immediate human sense also.

If, as the Christian learning body, we have to attend to the historical axis, we have no less to attend to the axis that spreads out from the Christian community to all men and to the cosmos itself, not in the sense that we are going to teach them, but that we are going to learn from them and learn with them. We are going to learn Jesus Christ from the Buddhists and the Hindus and the Moslems, and the post-Christians, and all the other varieties of non-Christians now and in the future and even in the past, because they too share the humanity of God. Confronting us in their very unbelief and unacceptance of Jesus Christ, they enable us to discover in them and in ourselves something more of the meaning of Jesus Christ. The scope of our learning is unlimited. It can be as particular as one likes; it can be as wide as one likes, although in the learning community of the Church one may have to specialise and select some way in which one can make more progress and contribute to the overall growth of the Church as the learning community.

H

This might appear to be the wistful dream of someone who is condemned to studying and learning anyway. It might appear that self-interest has prompted me to picture the Church in this way, and that what I am interested in is the *learned* community. There is a place certainly for learned men, in the accepted sense, within the community, if we are to keep these various lines open through which we can learn Jesus Christ. But the learned is always in danger of being arrogant; the learner is always called to be humble. The learned is somebody, in that awful phrase we sometimes use of the Church, who has the truth; the learner is one who seeks it. Think, for a moment, of the implications of that phrase: we have the truth. It means, in Christian terms, that we possess, own, and dispose of Jesus Christ. This is the kind of arrogance that is the very opposite of a learning community and a learning Church. It is the arrogance of the self-centred learned person or the arrogance of the self-centred teacher.

Learning, in my sense, is the growth in understanding of Jesus Christ which comes through this attentive listening to, communicating with and serving our fellow-men as the most effective and real presence of Christ in the world. In this process we will, I believe, be sanctified. It is in this kind of attention that we will be transformed; it is in this kind of attention, that we will also, if we follow it through, be crucified. Because the kind of surrender it demands is too much for most of us. We hedge our bets, build our barriers, protect ourselves from giving away too much of ourselves in this search. And one can understand this because we are only on the way and limping on the way. Yet, this is the process which will transform and sanctify us. If, however, the process is to be effective, it has to be in community and all the time, and for that we need leadership, leadership from one another. We ought all in this sense to be leaders and led. We are all eventually led by the Spirit, but at the human level this leading of the Spirit must express itself in different ways. I pick two ways which I think can apply to all of us.

One kind of leadership comes through what one may loosely

call inspiration or illumination. It is the leadership that derives from the person who has some kind of understanding he can communicate and which, in communicating, he also lives and which people can recognise and share and be aided by. We all know people like this. We have found them, I hope, at particular times in our lives—not very pretentious people, not even very significant people—perhaps a mother or a brother or a friend. This kind of leadership, this assistance and support in the learning process is of great importance, although it operates in a very unstructured way. At the moment it is very necessary in the Church to recognise its value—as well as its limitations.

One value I should like to comment further upon. It is my experience that I, and many people of my generation, the generation after me and the generation before me, in the course of their history, find that God has become totally obscured and that Jesus Christ has become meaningless. It is a common experience. It may be short-lived or it may last for a considerable time, but it is an experience that other people have shared with me, and that I can myself admit to. In this we need to be carried by others, supported by them. That is how they exercise leadership for us. The faith is the faith of the community. The learning is the learning of the community. The puzzlement and difficulty of one particular person is the responsibility of the community. Not that anybody wants to announce to the world at large his particular difficulty, but we should have some concept of how we may assist, support, and carry one another in this kind of difficulty. The carrying and support may not, as far as one can judge, lead on to a fuller, explicit belief in Jesus Christ, but it can lead on to something that implies that, and also to a fuller human existence for the particular person. But this inspiring and supporting role is one any of us may fulfil. It is leadership that may have a long-term aspect for particular people or may have a very short term, but it is the leadership we can all exercise and need from time to time.

There is a different kind of leadership, which is not so much assisting and supporting as creating situations in which one may listen, learn, communicate, serve. The creating of this kind of situation, of course, has been given to us, above all, in the eucharist. This is a situation which has been offered to the Church by Jesus Christ and in which this kind of listening, communicating and serving finds its deepest meaning, its ultimate source of power. We need a leadership that will create and ensure learning structures, by carrying on the basic learning structures, but by creating new ones too.

This is a view of the Church as a group called to learn Jesus Christ in all these various ways. The learning is a process at once passive and active, personal and communal, present, past and future. And it is in the light of its role in the world, not simply from the theological point of view, but also from the psychological point of view, the Church's most effective stance.

6

Dimensions of Vocation

Biblical Background

WE ARE all familiar with the call of Abraham, as well as the call of the people of Israel. We are also fairly familiar with the special call of the apostles or disciples by Christ, as well as the call of all Christians, in the sense that they are the assembly of the called, described as such by St Paul. We are very familiar with the idea of the relationship between God and mankind being structured about a call, and with the idea that the call of a particular person and a particular group is not for their own sake primarily, but for the sake of the wider group and ultimately for the sake of humanity. One point may be mentioned, which is evident as far as technical biblical evidence is concerned, but which might nevertheless be misleading : the word 'call' or 'vocation' in this sense is not applied to Jesus Christ. However, I think that the basic reality of vocation is expressed supremely in Christ, and it is to him that one must always return in any full discussion of the question.

The Meaning of Vocation

Before we go on to discuss the concept of the Church as the people called by God, and the role of particular peoples within the Church, I would like to say something about a more ultimate idea : the vocation structure of human existence. As human beings we each have a call, a call to be a particular individual human being. From the beginning of our existence,

born into a particular family at a particular time in a particular wider community at a certain period of history, we have
given to us on the one hand the elements whereby we can
become human beings, and on the other hand the call to use
these elements. Human existence is a matter of becoming a
human being: it is a call to become this particular human
being. The call presents itself to us in a whole series of different
ways, both in regard to long-term projects and in regard to
particular responses to particular situations. The kind of
human being we become is determined by the use we make of
the resources available to us. On the one hand we have the
gift, we have the resources to become a human being in the
course of our lives, and on the other hand we have the call or
invitation to use these resources. This kind of thinking influences much of the analysis of morality today. It is important
here because it means that all aspects of our lives, and all our
human endowments, are part at once of the gift we have and
of the task we have. This will be relevant to our discussions,
because we can think vainly of a primitive Church or of a
future Church, and forget that we have to deal actually with
the present Church and with the present people in that
Church. They provide the task and the resources.

The particular call which is embodied for us above all in
Jesus Christ, the call that enables us to say 'Our Father' to
God, cannot, of course, be reduced simply to the structures of
human existence. But it does seem that what is basic to human
existence, this gift and call, is now given a specification and
elevation in regard to mankind. We are called to be sons of
the Father, and brothers of one another, and this call of God
is an enabling call. The remarkable feature of the call in Jesus
Christ is that the 'come follow me' gives one at the same time
the capacity to follow him.

Within the human community as a whole this particular call
in the history of salvation goes back at least to Abraham
through the people of Israel. There is summed up in Jesus
Christ, and embodied in his presence in the world through the
Church, the elevation and specification of the total call of

mankind to be human. To be human in this precise way is to be human as sons of the Father.

We can, then, take the whole of human history and the human race as one large circle. All within that circle in fact have received this call from the Father to sonship, and this call is only possible because all within this circle have already a vocation-structure to their very existence. Inside that circle, we have the circle of people who enable us to see or understand the circle of the whole wider group : if in fact there weren't an Abraham and an Israel and a Jesus Christ, we would not be able to say that the whole of mankind was summoned or called in this way to be sons of the Father. The call of all mankind breaks surface, becomes specific, in the call of Abraham and of the people of Israel, and then, of course, above all in the climax of that in Jesus Christ. The Church is the concrete expression, the specification, of the Father's call of all men. It is the sacrament or sign of God's activity in the world, calling men to himself. They are all called and the structures of human existence are now specified by this invitation to be sons of the Father, but there is a particular group within which this call breaks surface, becomes perceptible. It is signified to us that this is in fact where Christ is manifest to the world. This means that the call which was manifest in Jesus Christ is now manifest and worked out through the presence of Christ in his visible Church throughout the world. The visible Church is essential to the world's self-understanding of its total call, and essential to its capacity to respond, because it is the presence of Christ in history. It is the Church as the assembly of the called that is the inner circle in our time.

In order that this inner circle or basic group may fulfil its purpose in the world, it needs certain structures, whereby the presence of Christ again appears above the surface. The two ways in which the presence of Christ does this are *word*, the preaching of the gospel, and *sacrament*. It is here that one sees more clearly what it means to be the assembly of the called. They are in fact the people who are summoned specifically by the word of God and have at the same time this call of God stamped on them in the sacraments of baptism and eucharist. It is in the word of God and in the administration of the sacraments that we can see more exactly that God by the medium of his Church is breaking through to mankind in the person of Jesus Christ.

The role of the Church is, then, through its listening to the word and celebration of the sacraments, to enable the wider world to understand itself, because it is only by understanding its God that it can understand itself. The Church is at the service of the world for the sake of the coming of God in men's hearts, for the sake of men discovering their own meaning and their own fulfilment as sons of the Father, for the sake of what we technically call the building of the kingdom. The Church is not the kingdom; the Church exists for the kingdom. The kingdom is something that is gradually being brought to fruition in the world at large. But we can only know this because the kingdom has broken through in Christ and in the Church.

The reason we need the two expressions, word and sacrament, which come together in Jesus Christ, is that in Jesus Christ the word of God is identified with human action and gesture and human living and human person, but for us what we say is not precisely what we live. There is always a gap in us between the word of God we announce and the word of God we live. If we had simply the word of God, it could appear very hollow, dependent perhaps on the personal oratorical gifts of the preacher or speaker, at least to the extent that we failed to reflect that this word of God is based on the person of Jesus Christ. In our Catholic tradition this is balanced by a sacramental activity which is also a ministry of the word, that is, of God's embodiment of himself in human action, in human communication. Here we can see the meaning of the *ex opere operato* dimension: that God acts in us, irrespective of the merits of the minister. These two traditions balance one another. The danger in Protestantism (which of course, has not entirely lost the sacramental tradition) is that one may depend to such an extent on the word that one will have good congregations only where one has good preachers. The danger in the Catholic tradition is that the emphasis on the efficacy of the sacrament will tend to a magical concept of sacrament. It is the balance between these two that enables us to bridge the gap which must exist in any other human being except Jesus Christ: that between the word of God as announced, and the word of God as expressed in living.

Through word and sacrament the Church exercises its proper mission in the world, that of enabling the world to understand and fulfil itself. All structures within the Church and all particular vocations in the Church exist to serve this mission. Within the Church, in the process of its attempting to serve its mission, certain structures have developed from basic elements which came to it from the first community of the called. From the beginning, there were different roles for different people in the Church, and these roles have varied considerably, but we have, in the course of some hundreds of years at any rate, settled into some particular roles which seem essential to the Church: the roles of the ministers of word and sacrament, bishop, priest and deacon.

The Church has another kind of structure, in the religious life, where you have word and sacrament presented in a rather different fashion. Here in fact the word and sacrament are presented not so much in what is said or done immediately, but in the style of life, as the sign manifest in the acceptance of the evangelical counsels or the vows. These are an announcement to the world of its call to the fulfilment of its true meaning. By the sacrifice for the kingdom of particular goods, in the context of forming a community, religious contribute a sign of the fulfilled community of mankind. This is an announcement of God's word to the world; it is also a sacrament, in the sense that it is an efficacious sign in so far as the community is true to its calling. It is an efficacious sign of God's presence to mankind forming a people for himself.

These are the two particular kinds of vocation to which we are accustomed, but they are vocations which simply specify the basic Christian vocation. Within these two, there can be a great many different varieties. You can have a teacher priest, a worker priest, as well as a parochial priest. You can have any kind of priesthood, as long as the ministry is given a clear relation to word and sacrament. Similarly, in regard to the religious life, you can have a vast variety. But I think that every kind of vocation of the Christian is, within the community of the Church at large, to bring the word of God to mankind and to celebrate the meaning and unity of mankind in the sacrament. These are the two essential services. Given the basic call to be a Christian, one has a rich variety of gifts derived from the vocation structure of human existence. With different personal gifts come different ways of being human. It would seem to me quite wrong to separate the vocation to be human, the vocation to be Christian, and the vocation to be religious or priest. The religious or priest is a particular kind of Christian, and he is this not because of any particular merits, and not because he is to be the recipient of any particular sanctification, but because he is called by God to fulfil a particular task for the rest of men, for the love of God and the love of neighbour. Christians in the community as a whole have a basic call to carry on the task of enabling mankind to understand at once its gift in Jesus Christ and the response this gift demands.

Fostering Vocations

There is not, it seems to me, any particular new mode of discerning what one is called to be by God, if one is a priest or religious. There is simply a new object, as it were, to which one is called, and that is the particular service, but the mode is in fact the rather traditional mode where, on the one hand, we are put into a situation where the service of the priesthood or the religious life appears to us as valuable and necessary for the Church and for mankind, and where we see this charge upon us as something that cannot be evaded but ought to be followed. As far as concerns the fostering of vocations all I would say is that in our offer of the priesthood to people, or our offer of the religious life, we have to beware of two positive dangers with their negative counterparts. We must, I think, stress that being a religious or a priest is not a denial but a fulfilment of our humanity. But we must not put this in the form one sometimes encounters among seminarians at present, that what counts is 'my personal development'. This is not what counts primarily, either for a human being or a Christian, for a religious or a priest. What counts is in fact my giving of myself to the others, both divine and human, and it is through this that human fulfilment comes. Even though the particular sacrifices involved in any way of life may be peculiar to that way of life, sacrifice is characteristic of all ways of life for people who would respond to others, and thus achieve personal fulfilment. We must on the one hand let people see that the way to be human is not eliminated by the priestly or the religious way of life; but that the way to be human and Christian involves sacrifice for everybody.

This is related to the second sort of positive and negative danger. I think we have a much better chance of getting people to accept Christianity and to accept vocation to the priestly or religious life if it is put forward as a life of sacrifice, instead of as a rather comfortable, educated, sophisticated kind of life. But again there is a very important negative side of this. We are frequently asking the wrong sacrifices and rather pointless sacrifices. The point about sacrifice is that it enables one to give oneself with all the resources one has to the service of God in others. We have to let our young people see that the sacrifices we ask have a point.

7

Human Relationships, Sexuality and Celibacy

ANY adequate treatment of the topic we are considering here would presuppose expertise and experience far beyond the range of the author and perhaps beyond any single individual's range. My approach is necessarily conditioned by my professional interest and experience, a moral theologian who is, in fact, a celibate by choice. The more precise meaning of these qualifications will, I hope emerge later.

I can at once outline my approach and summarise my position by saying that I regard the celibate state as a form of human relationship in the way I regard the married state; that I see it as having in common with all other human relationships a sexual dimension; and that I am naturally concerned as a Christian theologian with the Christian meaning of human relationships and their sexual dimension.

Human Relationship

A particular human relationship, which is my concern here, is a focusing of two people on one of their connections, but they exist in a series of overlapping connections which enter into their very constitutions. They are not separable from their social and historical contexts in this particular relationship. This model of 'human relationships' derives of course from my earlier analysis of morality as a human phenomenon. I may be pardoned for summarising the elements in that analysis relevant to the present discussion. In the concrete situation involving individuals or groups I see the moral obligation, or, as I prefer to describe it, the moral call affecting both poles, as a summons to mutual recognition, respect and the further concrete response appropriate to the particular situation.

When I press the implications of this model I find that underlying the call is the notion of the human participants as gift to one another. And the gift-call structure (in my model) operates at the various levels of human existence or in its various dimensions.

Here I am confronted with what seems an equally inescapable component of that model of the human interchange. Gift-call must be balanced by the fact that men are also threat-provoking-fear and may be experienced as such in any situation.

The threat element cannot be easily explained or overcome. It betrays a failure collectively and individually to *recognise* one another as gift and so to *respect* and *respond*. It cannot be entirely eliminated from human relationships; but the moral call, which I have spelled out in three moments as recognition, respect and response, involves a deeper call to allow gift to predominate over threat. This deeper call then enters into each of the more specific calls; it requires continuous positive response although this will be for the most part implicit; such positive response does not finally eliminate the threat element any more than continuous negative response finally eliminates the gift element in our human moral encounters; it may issue in a predominant moral stance and its implied life-style which will then be normally expressed in a reaction to others in the particular situation. These others will in accordance with the predominant and basic stance be treated predominantly as gift or threat.

The human being in relationship has a historical as well as a social dimension. As individual or group the relating subject in the present bears interiorly the past in experience and reaction to experience while he confronts the future. All human relationships have a time dimension; they are in process, developing or declining. Man's continuity with the universe is a basic condition of his human existence and his capacity for relationship. History should not be reduced to evolution, biological or sociological, but the conditions for human decision and the development based on it cannot escape man's cosmic situation and the physical/biological components together with their psychological/sociological counterparts which form a constitutive element in him.

Man-in-relationship is man-in-community-in-history-in-cosmos. He is the subject to be considered in any particular relationship. Neglect of any one of these factors or their treatment as accidental modifications and not constitutive elements, obscures or distorts one's understanding of the relationship. One or other element may be more emphasised at any one time but they are all relevant all the time. In considering the gift-call combined with the threat-fear structure of the relationship, these different dimensions of human existence, which may be distinguished but never separated, all play an important role. That the relationship should develop morally, the persons or groups involved are called to identify and promote the gift aspect at the expense of the threat.

The identification and promotion of the gift aspect at the expense of the threat may be re-expressed as the *recognition* of the other (individual/group) in his true otherness (realised and potential); the respecting of that otherness in its unique character as a (real and potential) centre of understanding and feeling, deciding, acting and loving; and the *response* to that other in the channel established by a particular context or situation. Other-recognition is at the same time self-identification; other-respect involves self-acceptance; other-response appropriate to the situation involves self-development even to the extent of self-creation by bringing into realisation aspects of the self which were hitherto only potential and perhaps not even recognised as such. Critical situations and the demands involved reveal and realise potentialities which one may never have suspected that one had. It is in the process of other-recognition/self-identification, other-respect/self-acceptance, and other-response/self-creation that the mutual enrichment of other and self can take place and the mutual threat be diminished.

The Sexual Dimension

What, then, are the implications for sexuality of what I have been saying?

The man-in-relationship earlier discussed as man-in-community-in-history-in-cosmos is sexually determined as male or female. This does not apply simply to him as a cosmic being in continuity with the physical, or more specifically biological world. His sexuality is also an aspect of his social and historical characters; of man therefore in his full relational capacity and actuality. The sexual differentiation cannot be reduced to biology any more than biology can be ignored. The social-historical situation provides the matrix in which the biological is personalised, that is, plays its constitutive role in the emergence and development of the particular and unique world of this man or this woman. It is not merely a qualifying role but a constitutive one for the person himself and for all his relationships. Some important general consequences follow from this.

In himself and in all his relationships the person is sexual. He cannot behave or regard himself as if he could abstract from his sexuality. In reacting or meeting with others he/she is always man or woman. The interaction always reflects this, even in situations in which the medium of exchange seems quite remote. I always feel differently and, I think, behave differently when addressing a single-sex audience as compared with a mixed one, or when addressing men as compared with women and this even on such neutral matters as the relation of St Ambrose's *De Officiis* to Cicero's. In such situations the biological-sexual interpreted in the sense of genital does not appear, but the biological in its social-historical (cultural) character, as part of self, does. What *kind* of 'part of self' is further determined by the identification, acceptance and creation of self as a sexual being which has already been achieved. In the light of the earlier analysis of relationship this sexual self-appropriation depends on the recognition of, respect for and response to the other as a sexual being which occurs in the history of one's relationships. The sexual aspect of these relationships varies as I have said from relationship to relationship and from situation to situation but it is inescapable. This should not lead one to regard it primarily as a burden or a threat. Indeed, according to my position, it is primarily gift or ought to be. The permanent call in this area of human relating as in all others is to enable the gift to triumph over the threat, although the one can never entirely eliminate the other.

Chastity is to be defined then as the virtue whereby one's sexuality in relationship operates predominantly as gift and not as threat. It can do this if one recognises the other in his/her sexuality as gift and so identifies the self sexually; if one respects the other sexually and so accepts the self; if one responds to the other in his/her sexual condition with the response appropriate to the particular situation and so creates or develops the self. The chaste person is the one who integrates his sexual endowment/gift into his relationship in this way, not the one who seeks to repress or ignore it. This will be his predominant tendency but not his exclusive one. There will always be admixture of threat and self-centredness conflicting with gift and other-centredness. And one may move from one predominant tendency or basic stance to another in the sexual area as much as in any other. Chastity then is a continuing call to recognise, develop and integrate one's sexuality in the love and service of others. It is not something one has and (with luck) hangs on to, but a life-task.

So far I have been treating sexuality as a general component of all human relationships, which it is. It is necessary to apply what I have said (however briefly and inadequately) to two obvious categories of human sexual relationship in which sexuality finds a more specific expression. Marriage is naturally considered the primary relationship in the discourse. My observations here may omit much that is said better elsewhere while I concentrate on aspects which arise from my own approach to human relationships. In marriage sexuality is also both gift and threat. One does not need very much experience of marriage difficulties to realise how threatening the sexual-genital relationship itself may be or how enriching it may also be in face of other difficulties. And the gift aspect is not easily, quickly and fully realised. It involves a continuing call and response. As a human and sexual relationship marriage is or ought to be continually becoming and developing. It provides a life-task. And it is not an isolated atomic relationship divorced from the whole series of overlapping relationships with their sexual dimensions in which everybody lives. Again, it may be that too much emphasis is placed on the exclusivity of the marriage relationship in its sexual connotation, ignoring the sexual (admittedly different) connotation of all one's human relationships. The uniqueness of marriage sexually should not lead one to ignore the wider sexuality of all human relationships.

Celibacy is also a human and sexual relationship, at least in the general sense of qualifying one's relationships sexually in a particular way. In its more conventional presentation, whether in terms of 'eunuchs for the kingdom of God' (*Matt.* 19:12) or of nuns as 'brides of Christ' the emphasis was on the 'relationship to God'. It is perhaps one more (overdue) example of how we have begun to translate 'God-talk' into 'man-talk' but it does not need to have the reductionist consequences which some such translations involve. Whatever its fashionableness the procedure will in this instance, I hope, lead to a more careful consideration of the full meaning of Christian celibacy, including its 'relationship to God' dimension.

If celibacy constitutes a particular way of relating to people it will enter into all the celibate's relationships in some way. One is free to relate and so to love but one is not free for a particular kind of sexual relationship, marriage or its equivalent. The surrender of this particular freedom cannot eliminate the wider sexual dimension of all one's relationships and does not release one from the obligation of identifying, accepting, developing and integrating one's sexuality in recognising, respecting and responding to the other. As celibacy is freedom

I

to love in its own way, it is freedom to love sexually as there is no other human form of loving and relating. The surrender of marriage provides a new context and so a different freedom for love but that must not be divorced from the permanent sexual character of man. Here, too, sexuality operates in relationship in accordance with the gift-threat structure. Just as one might easily conclude that sexuality in marriage was all gift, so one might conclude that in celibacy it was all threat. For all the differences in context and in expression, the task for the celibate also remains one of enabling the gift to triumph over the threat, and it is a life-task. Celibacy as a form of chastity is not something one has, but something one must (painfully) achieve through the process of love and service in which one's sexuality finds its particular expression.

Christian Significance

I do not presume to offer any developed and comprehensive Christian understanding of the human phenomenon of sexuality. In line with the understanding of human relationships which I have outlined, I would draw attention to the necessity here as elsewhere of understanding human sexuality as a Christian, by attending as fully as possible to the human phenomenon and then seeking a deeper interpretation in the light of creation, incarnation, salvation and consummation as understood in Jesus Christ.

That fuller attention to the phenomenon of sexuality places it firmly in the discussion of man-in-relationship as person, man-in-community-in-history-in-cosmos, involved in gift-threat interchange with his fellow-man. How the doctrines listed above confirm and interpret more deeply this understanding of man may be indicated very briefly. Creation and incarnation reveal the depth of the gift character of this person, in continuity with the cosmos and part of it, yet endowed with a dignity above the rest of the cosmos, which has divine origin and significance. This particular dignity not only involves some special relationship to God but hinges on the capacity for human relationship itself and is directly connected with sexual differentiation and love (*Gen.* 1, 2). The social context of all relations—which are, of course, socially constitutive themselves —pervades the whole of God's dealings with mankind in the Judaeo-Christian tradition. That tradition itself is a history which is given its guarantee of meaning as well as its thrust and power in the consummation already realised in Jesus Christ but still to be accomplished in time by men. The pervasiveness of the threat to this accomplishment, the threat which all men are to one another, becomes in this understanding the universality of sin. The present and ultimate triumph of gift over threat is the achievement of Jesus Christ extended to the rest of us by the presence of the Spirit. Human relationships in their sexual character as gift and threat are assured this saving power of Christ, to the extent indeed that the Catholic Church speaks of the most distinctive and critical of human relationships from the sexual aspect—marriage—as a sacrament.

The crucial way of salvation, of the triumph of gift over threat and of the fruitful, loving unity of mankind, must not be obscured. The other-centredness which is demanded in all relationships and assumes intimate depth in marriage, remains, in a world also characterised by threat and self-centredness, a way of dying to self, often in a painful manner. It remains a way of the cross. In quite a different fashion the loving life of the celibate is exposed to the danger of selfishness only to be overcome by his taking the cross as it is offered to him. As far as cross-bearing is concerned and precisely in the area of sexuality, there seems no compelling reason to believe that the married will get off more lightly than the celibate. In the world of gift and threat, however, the celibate's surrender of the fulfilment of one aspect of his gift can, in combination with the married's affirmation of that fulfilment precisely as gift for others, and in the context of joyful generous community service, bear witness to the power of God in Christ as he invites all men to enjoy the consummation already achieved in Christ.

8

Nationalism and the Christian

AT a conference in the United States a couple of years ago I was asked: 'Are you proud to be an Irishman?' My answer 'No' caused some dismay among my audience, especially the Irish-American members, which was only partly allayed by my comment that I did not see any more virtue in 'national pride' than in personal pride. For myself the occasion proved both an expression of and a stimulus to the rethinking which I realised the whole problem of nationalism demanded in today's world.

The more horrific results of a certain kind of nationalism at any rate, appear daily on our television screens from the Middle East and the Far East, from Southern Africa and Northern Ireland. The revulsion we feel coupled with the dreamy talk of one world, a single global village, made possible for us by technology may suggest an instant, simple and definitive 'Yes' to the question sometimes posed: Is nationalism outmoded? It may well be the correct answer but more careful consideration is needed if it is not to join other instant but disposable answers in the litter-bin of history.

Nationalism as we commonly, if rather imprecisely, speak of it is a relatively recent phenomenon. Of course it can trace its roots far back into prehistory and these roots broke surface in a particular way in the Jewish tradition to which Christianity and the western world is so much indebted. Yet the nationalism which now confronts us developed in the nineteenth century with its immediate roots in the American and French revolutions. It was this kind of nationalism which dominated much of the settlement at the end of World War I and came back to haunt Europe in the '-isms' which led to World War II as well as in the break-down of colonialism in Africa and Asia in subsequent decades.

The imprecision I adverted to above reflects the diversity of forms in which nationalism has developed even in the world in which it was born, Europe and North America, without taking account of the necessarily richer diversity offered by South America, Africa and Asia. This diversity of form might be categorised in several different ways. One of the most significant ways takes as its starting-point the critical relation between nationalism and politics, between nation and state. I call this the critical relation because it is the combination of national identity and political aspiration or achievement which has been such a potent influence for life and death in the last couple of centuries. To say this is not to ignore other very potent influences, perhaps even more potent ones in terms of class, racial or economic discrimination and inequality. It is not to offer a comprehensive analysis of the changing map of the world from 1775 to 1975. I simply wish to emphasise one important and almost pervasive influence, with which no doubt other influences were inextricably mixed; and an influence which at certain times in certain countries took precedence over all others. My own country, Ireland, has been one example of this at various times in its recent history.

In a crude simplification of the two types of nationalism I have in mind, distinguished by their different starting-points, it might be said of the one that the state precedes the nation and attempts to create it, while in the other the nation precedes the state and attempts to create it. In an even cruder exemplification of this principle it might be said that the United States of America belongs to the first category (to be followed eventually by a United States of Europe?) and that Ireland belongs to the second : that Category I is an Anglo-Saxon form with its 'typical' pragmatic bias and Category II is a Celtic-European form with its 'typical' romantic or ideological bias. Without descending to the level of comic-strip caricature in regard to particular nations or states, the predominance of one or other starting-point, with definite implications for understanding and practice, can be discerned in recent history.

The more pragmatic starting-point stresses the right of a people to manage their own affairs. The people's right to self-determination or self-government free of outside overlords or interference is still a very potent force in world politics. The development of democracy has contributed to this demand for government from within. The people in Category I tend to define themselves geographically rather than ethnically or culturally or historically. They wish to constitute a state of their own on a territorial definition primarily. Combined with the drive towards self-government, and perhaps inspiring and overriding it, there may be economic interests where the external government is considered to be exploiting the people of the area. In the pursuit of 'home rule' the ambitions for power of particular individuals or groups will frequently play an important role. With the achievement of statehood or self-government much greater attention is paid to cultural identity and unity, to the development of a new ethnic reality (e.g. the American), to the factors which characterise the starting-point of Category II of the nation-states.

While various ethnic, cultural, religious and historical factors played a highly significant role in political developments from the tribe to the empire and were recognised as doing just that, it was again in the nineteenth century that a self-conscious drawing together of these factors led to a definition of the people as a nation in the current sense. The unity and identity of the people as a nation, the partially mystical discussion of the 'soul' of the nation by German philosophers such as Herder or Irish revolutionaries such as Pearse, preceded but inevitably demanded independent statehood for every nation. The Treaty of Versailles embodied a brave attempt to align political and national boundaries in Europe. It was the high-point of the nation-state of Category II.

In distinguishing Categories I and II in this way I have been, as I said, drastically simplifying. However justified the distinction may be in discussing immediate starting-points for particular nation-states, subsequent history tends to diminish the difference considerably. The state finds the development of a national unity and identity useful as a cohesive force; national unity and identity seek expression in independent statehood. It is nationalism as a political force, antecedent and subsequent to political independence which demands fresh analysis and evaluation.

The birth of a nation is usually an obscure historical process, at least where nation precedes state. Two elements may, however, be discussed as operative in both categories, some historical process whereby a particular group of people can discern a certain unity and identity for themselves and some decision to separate themselves from neighbouring groups. This decision may be well-prepared in an implicit or informal way. At a certain stage in development it will become fully articulated in the claim to separate nationhood and independent statehood. It is only with the explicit articulation that the self-consciousness of the nation, its sense of identity and unity, its awareness of its past history and origin as well as its present and future roles, develops into what may properly be called nationalism.

Conscious identity then of being a distinct people in relation to the surrounding peoples is one of the essential characteristics of the 'nation'. This identity has a certain affinity with the identity which the individual may experience as a person. It is important however to examine the factors which may contribute to this sense of identity as a people and not to fall into the trap of assuming that they are the same as or even very similar to those contributing to personal identity. While the genesis of 'national identity' may differ considerably from one nation to another and in particular between nations belonging to Category I and Category II, some of the same contributing factors combine in varying ways to form national identity in each case.

An obvious factor in many instances is the geographical one. Shared territory can play an important role in the development of a people with a conscious identity. It normally provides the context in which other factors get an opportunity to emerge. In the self-consciousness associated with the achievement of or aspiration towards statehood it plays a significant role. Natural boundaries do not of themselves constitute nations and the eventual state-boundaries which operate on the major land masses owe little enough to great natural dividing points. A fixed territory, however it may have been fixed, is characteristic of most peoples in their claim to nationhood.

At this 'natural' level one might also list the biological or racial component in nationality. It has, however, been given much more emphasis in philosophising about nationality and has had significant and dangerous influence in practice. The appeal to 'blood' as exemplified in Nazism or any of the contemporary manifestations of 'racialism' from Southern Africa to North America has shown a destructive power which has also proved dangerously contagious. And the danger is not diminished by the absurdity of basing human rights on 'biological purity', a purity which it has proved impossible in practice to establish or maintain.

The 'natural' factors of biology and geography ('Blut und Boden') do not always play such a significant role in national identity. When they do, their very sub-human and sub-rational character make them particularly difficult to control. Even this century alone provides sufficient evidence for that.

At the 'human' as distinct from the 'natural' level, the nation is formed by shared human experience, in achievement and failure. The struggle for survival in face of natural hostility of land or sea or climate or of the human hostility of more powerful neighbours, with the shared victories and defeats, creates a shared awareness which, with time and time's conscious recorder, memory, becomes self-consciousness, the group's awareness of itself as a distinct group. It may take a particularly powerful prophetic voice or a whole series of voices for this self-consciousness to grow to a sense of identity which of itself provides the people with a vision for its future, an effective aspiration towards that future, and creates the energy to seek and achieve it. Through the nineteenth and twentieth centuries the shared experiences of many groups have found the voices and so the vision, aspiration and energy in the phenomenon called nationalism. In the emergence of nationalism the experiences themselves were more subtly understood and evoked in their cultural expression.

The shared experiences inevitably issue in a shared pattern of living. Food, clothing, housing reflect the common needs and resources available to a particular group. And ways of acquiring and using these display a parallel similarity. In work and in play the group defined by a common history and geography exhibit their common identity at first unconsciously —but in response to particular critical events or personalities, more and more consciously.

The most obvious and in so many ways the most powerful expression of the people's common way of life or shared experience is their language. Language became in the nineteenth century a touchstone of nationalism and has remained so in many places through the twentieth. In the nineteenth century the great Germanic movement took the German language as badge of national identity; Thomas Davis, leader of the Young Ireland movement and editor of the influential paper *The Nation*, coined a phrase which became a slogan with his 'A nation without a language is only half a nation'; in the twentieth the founders of the state of Israel have attached great importance to the restoration of Hebrew as a national language; and the rulers of so many modern states from Belgium to India have to cope with the national divisions threatened by different languages.

Related to language and expressive of the shared way of life are the 'high culture' achievements of a people in literature, art and music. They constitute high-points in the human achievement of a people which in turn can inspire further achievements of a similar kind or fertilise quite different areas of activity such as the political. 'Folk culture' activities may be more closely related to the generality of the people and embody more of their distinctive characteristics. The national consciousness as it develops depends on the vitality of this cultural life, folk and high.

A common and sometimes crucial factor in cultural and national identity has been religion. In intent, religion comprehends for a particular individual and group at once the most comprehensive and profound understanding of self. It sets the individual and people in relation to the universe as a whole, its ultimate good and truth in the supreme being, and so creates the basis and context for relations between individuals and groups. It is easy to see how, where religion is an active force, it will enter deeply and pervasively into a people's identification of itself as a particular people in opposition to others. This in fact did happen in the course of history and we are still struggling with some of the consequences of it. However, in nineteenth-century Europe as nationalism waxed religion as a social force of this kind waned. Indeed nationalism tended to replace religion for many people and the national wars of the nineteenth century to replace the religious of the sixteenth. Yet religion remains distinctive of peoples and a constituent feature of nations in many states from Northern Ireland to Pakistan, however this association may benefit or even be compatible with the tenets of the particular religion.

Such a crude survey of the 'human' factors operative in the formation of a distinctive people with a consciousness of themselves as distinct may give a false impression of the inevitability or automatic character of the development of nationalism. Human decision and responsibility are involved of broadly two kinds; initiating and accepting. The initiating activity may be diffuse and cumulative, involving a wide range of people over a considerable period, or attributable to a small number of creative-prophetic people at a particular period, or to any combination of these two. The acceptance may be more or less active or passive. The initiative of the few will not be effective without the acceptance, at least passive, of the many.

The development or even eventual survival of national identity or the traditions which form it require the positive affirmation of the people themselves. A passively inherited tradition is not adequate to the fluidly communicating world in which all men live today. Decision and responsibility bear on national identity its development or decline.

Historically, decision and affirmation of national identity have tended to become absorbed in the search for statehood or, where the state exists, in its further development. Although nationhood has in theory rested on pre- or a-political factors just discussed, in practice they were frequently subordinated to political ends. The democratic right of self-determination was identified with the right of the nation to be an independent state. In many instances this was a good practical solution; in some instances it was the only protection of a cultural minority or the most effective way of allowing people to live peaceably together. Yet the results politically were not always so happy either for the new minorities or the peaceful co-existence of the new states. The close association of national identity and political independence proved a very powerful and sometimes destructive force. It is this force that is properly called nationalism. It is in the development and exercise of this force that much of the national self-consciousness affirmed itself and used its decisive influence in the nineteenth and twentieth centuries.

Just as national identity did not spring from and does not coincide with political structure or achievement and yet became closely associated with it, a weaker but similar relationship developed between national groupings and socio-economic structures, aspirations, achievements. Many movements for what became national as well as political independence whether in North America or North Africa were inspired at least partly by reaction to economic and social exploitation. The national consciousness among black Americans today has obvious social and economic roots. The 'third world' is having its consciousness continuously raised in terms which are not simply social and economic but contain strong elements of the nationalism we have known over the last century. Europe's nation-states set a headline in economic nationalism from which many of these 'third-world' states are suffering and learning. Where economic and social interests reinforced national feeling, as they did in so many colonial countries, the movement towards political independence in nationalist terms was greatly strengthened. On the other hand where 'socialism' sought to promote the 'social well-being' in defiance of national feeling, it has had often to be imposed and maintained with the aid of the 'big battalions'. National identity and feeling as it has developed cuts across class identity and feeling. In cases where conflict prevails, such national identity and feeling may depend on a great many other factors.

Even this sketchy description of the human phenomenon of nationalism as it has developed over two hundred years should help us to answer in a more considered way the question implied in the title of this chapter. The evaluation of the phenomenon and hence the answer to the question has an ethical as well as a political dimension; it demands a consideration of value as well as of fact or consequences. More accurately the ethical is embodied in the political; the value is inextricably bound up with the facts. I shall attempt therefore to assess the positive and negative achievements of historic nationalism in a necessarily general way and at the same time draw out the values involved. I should then wish to add a comment from the perspective of the Christian believer in the hope of offering some helpful overall comment on how our question is to be answered.

National consciousness undoubtedly draws attention to the human achievements of the locality and community into which the individual is born, achievements on which he depends for his development as person-in-community. The more conventional description of man as a social being may be more fully understood by using the term person-in-community. The specifically human aspects of his social condition are at least indicated and the hyphenated structure calls attention to the complex interrelation which exists between the individual person and the social grouping(s) in which he comes into existence and develops. Persons are formed in and by communities; communities are formed by and of persons. The early predominance of community over person yields (ideally) to a more balanced relationship in which the adult person, while incorporating much of what the community has to offer in language for example or style of life or ethical, aesthetic political or religious value, and still relying on the resources and services of the community in these and other matters, reaches a certain maturity and autonomy which allows him to critically evaluate and select from among the received values and at the same time contribute creatively himself to the pattern of behaviour, the vision and the values of the community. It is this autonomous evaluation and personal creation which ensures the continuing vitality of the community, as well as the human fulfilment of the person. The evaluation and creation can vary enormously in degree and kind. Yet it must not be regarded as the privilege of the few exceptionally talented. In language, for instance, conversation that is really alive and personal is a creative activity and novelists and dramatists frequently draw on this in their own creative activity. Synge, O'Casey and Behan, to take a couple of relevant Irish examples, illustrate in their acknowledged dependence on local expression how language and life are enriched by people usually regarded as educationally and so linguistically deprived. The more formal attention to folk culture and later sophisticated studies in anthropology and linguistics continue to reveal the vital and creative role of 'ordinary' people in community achievement.

The 'nationalist' movement focused attention on the human achievement of the particular group. It opened people to the value of the tradition created and so enabled them to appreciate and appropriate that tradition in human fashion as a source of identity and security and as a basis for their future development. In this sense it produced an awareness of roots which could be nurtured for further growth. As given to the new members of the community and as enriching for them, the national tradition could be properly described as gift. Yet it was gift which made certain demands, which embodied a certain call to understand and to so receive the gift in human and not automatic fashion; to develop it and contribute to it. Otherwise the particular individuals and parent community would not be enriched or vitalised by the tradition; the wider human community would gradually lose the vital force of the particular community's achievement. For the sake of that wider human community whose vitality depends on the smaller for the sake of each of its members and for the sake of its community life, individuals and particular communities have a responsibility for the health of their particular traditions as human achievements. In a world of 'mass' communications and 'mass' culture—and I understand the word 'mass' in the dual sense of universality and lacking real human participation by the many—this responsibility may be at once more acute, more difficult to recognise discriminatingly and almost impossible to discharge.

It would be naïve to suppose that even at the cultural level national consciousness has operated as pure gift. Like all human phenomena it has proved ambiguous, resulting in good and evil. It has been threat as well as gift, destructive as well as creative. The destructive element has certainly operated in the cultural field. However, it has been the association of the cultural with the political that has been proved particularly pernicious. The struggle for and development of the nation-state made people conscious of their distinctiveness as a people and of the human achievement embodied in that distinctiveness. It underlined the gift that was theirs and the call it embodied. Yet the internal and external consequences for the people too frequently included seriously destructive elements.

Internally to the nation-state, minority cultures received little recognition or encouragement. The principle on which the state was erected or which it espoused, of political self-determination for culturally distinct communities, could not cope with the small or scattered minority groups within the confines of the state itself. Mono-cultural states, as the nation states tended to be, could be genuinely oppressive therefore as far as minorities were concerned. By a strange irony, the establishment of a particular culture as the national one was not always to its benefit either. Cultural establishment by the state, like religious establishment, proved at best a mixed blessing. Neither cultural vitality nor religious vitality can be commanded by law. Of course in some instances cultural and religious establishment are combined. The resultant possibility of discrimination or oppression of the minority is doubled; the deadly potential for majority beliefs and life-pattern correspondingly increased. In the struggle for independence the association of national awareness and political aspiration might be an enormous source of vitality; in the subsequent organisation of independence achieved it could become so easily fixated and embattled that it both opposed other cultures in its own state and slowly destroyed itself. In discussing the threat posed by the national consciousness in the nation state I have ignored the more terrifying racialist consequences which were referred to above, not because they are not found quite frequently and in association with nationalism (the names of two most notable exponents of these—the National Socialists in Hitler's Germany and the Nationalists in modern South Africa—are evidence of this), but because they are so obviously terrifying that it is scarcely necessary to discuss them.

In external relations, national consciousness and nationalism have proved the occasion of international war or intensified the reasons for it. At a less obviously destructive level they have, through economic nationalism, helped to create—or certainly to perpetuate—economic wars and exploitation. In the search for peace with justice which is the great challenge of our own time, national feeling and the self-interest it promotes have proved serious obstacles. A cultural isolationism or xenophobia does not ultimately promote the life of the national culture. For that a healthy appreciation of others and interchange with them is necessary. Otherwise the particular culture and indeed all particular cultures are liable to be increasingly replaced by superficial and impoverished universal life, thought and language styles, which even now threaten us.

Historic nationalism has been both gift and threat, liberating at many different levels of human existence as well as imprisoning. It has undoubtedly helped many individuals and groups to develop on the basis of the resources and achievements of their own place and people. It has also frustrated further development in many instances and at many levels. Clearly the obligation of the individual and the group is to exercise discrimination between gift and threat and work so that gift triumphs over threat. The past is irrevocable but one can choose to encourage certain forces which emerge from it and discourage others. The national experience is irrevocable for many people but one can choose which of its achievements one wants to build on. In many ways that is already taking place today. However, without conscious attention to both gift and threat elements, the development may be more powerfully ambiguous or the whole national experience may be discarded as useless.

In the thrust towards internationalism which is apparent in communications, cultural patterns of all kinds, economics and politics, nationalism as we have known it is a waning force. This is not to ignore that very many peoples have not known this experience at all yet or else they have been awakened to it very recently. For them it may be expected to exercise a very potent attraction still. However, in the planetary situation in which we now live the nationalist stage of politics, economics and cultural achievement is hardly likely to prove adequate. The question is what should replace it; how should we develop from here on? Will the gift and enriching aspects of national identity, consciousness and achievement, be used as a base for further growth or will the threatening elements so overshadow them that an easy and empty universalism will emerge and be accepted. The ambiguities of world- or at least continental-size states are no less threatening than those of nationalism. Because of the change in scale they may be even more so. I have no doubt that peaceful development of the world for all men is at once an ethical imperative and a historical opportunity. It will take time and energy and above all direction.

Yet it could be left directionless and create global problems where we had relatively localised ones. Indeed this has to some extent already happened. The gifts of the various peoples and places must be respected as the nationalist movement at its best taught us, but they must be integrated with those of their neighbours in an organic, vital and ultimately world-wide community or rather community of communities. The rootlessness of the universalist way of life which is already with us, combined with the ruthlessness of international business even more with us, could make the human destruction wrought by a 'diseased' nationalism seem relatively slight. In the emergence of a better world the nationalist phenomenon can be recognised as a stage of development. For the western world it would appear to be outmoded. It has become a stage of arrested development. The values which it uncovered in the historical achievements of the particular communities, in the rich diversity of human living throughout the planet, can and should be accepted as permanently important in the development of some wider and hopefully richer political and cultural context.

The Christian perspective on the nationalism phenomenon suggests a more radical assessment. The positive evaluation of the community achievement in different fields is reinforced by the doctrines of creation and incarnation. Human realisation of the potential of the world at once confirms and collaborates with the work of the Creator God and in the light of the incarnation renders that God more fully accessible in the world. The basic gift or grace of man and his world embodies a call which urges on man cultural and political tasks which the nation has historically in part at least accomplished. The gift or grace which is by Christians finally attributable to God the Creator is seen in its fullness in Jesus Christ as involving an intimate sharing in the power and glory and life of God himself. In him all creation strains after its fullness (*Rom.* 8); at the head and climax of creation men are called to be and are sons of the Father, sharers in the divine nature itself. The fulfilment for all in the kingdom of God is to be sought in history but will be finally attained in the absolute future which

K

lies beyond history. In that seeking, with its ultimate and divine implications, the human achievements of each individual and group, of each nation, receive a final significance.

Not that Christian belief implies any naïve optimism about human progress or ignores the ambiguities of history, the threat as well as the gift in every human situation and accomplishment. The doctrines of creation and incarnation take a very realistic view of evil in the world. (For some Christians this presence of evil has entirely dominated their vision of the world.) Incarnation becomes redemption, a buying back by Jesus Christ through the divine power which was in him of man and creation from powers of evil or sin. It becomes salvation and liberation. What creation had to offer for man's fulfilment would be used by him to his destruction were it not for the power and availability of God in Jesus Christ. Fixation in particular stages of human achievement which has been such a threatening feature of nationalism among other human phenomena is one of the commonest manifestations of human weakness revealed in all its depth through Jesus Christ and overcome by him.

The self-centredness, arrogance and self-aggrandisement to which nationalism has frequently led are understood in Christian terms as aspects of man's continuing sinfulness. Born into a nation caught up in this nationalist passion, the individual is infected with mankind's sinfulness also in this fashion. For him what has been traditionally called original sin is partly expressed in such a form. The further evil consequences of this closed nationalism in oppression at home or war and exploitation abroad embody that sinfulness which the Bible so frequently describes in terms of hostile division between man and God, between man and man, within each individual man or group. And it is this division which has been overcome in the death and resurrection of Jesus Christ. In Paul's words, reflecting on the more obvious divisions in his own time, there is no longer Jew or Greek, slave or free, male or female (*Gal.* 4). All are one in Christ, as sons of the Father and brothers of one another. The basic unity of the human race which is at once gift and task, already given and still to be achieved, is placed for the Christian beyond all possibility of question and set on its ultimate basis. In this perspective national boundaries may be useful stages of development but they can be no more. The Christian summons is now to a fuller realisation of the community of all men by harnessing the resources of all and of the world at large. In the halting ambiguous achievements of such a world-wide community, the gift and call finally manifest in Jesus Christ receive fuller expression; the kingdom which he preached and which his Father had given into his hands moves towards its fulfilment. No nation or closed nationalism may impede the march of God's kingdom. At the level of the human tasks, political and cultural, which now confront us and at the level of their Christian significance, nationalism at least for the 'developed' world can be seen to be inadequate and outmoded.

9

Human Violence:
A Question of Ethics or Salvation

The Human Agent as Subject

PERHAPS human violence was even more widespread in the past. The present concern may be based on expansion of communications, the horrifying possibilities of the weapons available and our crumbling illusions about the growth of civilisation. Without invoking for the moment any of the current explanations of the violence from the ethological to the theological, it is necessary to recognise its pervasiveness and the threat it poses for human living, immediately and directly in so many places, mediately and indirectly every place.

The violence in question is that for which man is responsible, the destruction or damage wrought by man on his fellow-man or human property. The responsibility is human. The agent of destruction is man himself. Human violence is not to be confused with natural catastrophes or 'acts of God'. However one finally evaluates the degree of responsibility of the human agent, there is a human agent to which the violence can in some sense be attributed. Only in this sense can violence be said to be an ethical question. Only in so far as man recognises human responsibility for violence, at least through negligence, can he hope and try to remedy it. In human affairs the acceptance of responsibility is not primarily directed to apportioning blame but to recognising and promoting the possibility of achievement. Unless man has some responsibility for the violence which exists there is no point in his talking about trying to eliminate it.

The human agent concerned may be an individual. Violence by one individual to another in the home or the school as well as on the streets is so usual as scarcely to merit comment. In discussing most moral issues it is easier to concentrate on the individual as agent. Analysis of moral responsibility confines itself to the individual even where he is recognised as a member of a group. The individual remains the irreducible centre of moral awareness and decision. Yet so many acts of violence are carried on by groups, large and small, whose corporate awareness and decision are not readily reducible to the discrete individuals and their awareness and decisions, that here as in other moral discussions, special attention must be paid to group awareness and responsibility in their peculiar group-character. Indeed the more intractable problems of violence from Northern Ireland to Southern Africa involve to a very large extent group awareness and decision. Unless one is prepared to grapple with the complexities of the group as moral agent, many of the problems of violence (and of life in general) will have to be ignored.[1]

The Object of Violence

If man, as individual or group, is the relevant agent of violence, the moral subject, whose responsibility must be out-lined, then the object of his violence has its own complexities. Primarily and indeed ultimately it is his fellow-man, as individual or group : primarily because the first and certainly the important victim of violent activity is people; ultimately because however indirect the relationship between damaged property and any particular people may be, it finally counts as damage because of how it affects people. The violence of the home or the streets or the battlefield is clearly destroying

1. Cf. *chapter 2*, pp. 20-23 and *chapter 3*, 'The Moral Subject', above for fuller discussion of the group as moral subject.

people. Allowing for the twenty-minute warnings so that the buildings can be evacuated before the guerrilla bombs explode or for the successful attempt to attack only military installations or strategic industries, the property damage rebounds on people, otherwise it would not be any use as a weapon of war. Violent struggle is always between men, so that the concentration of property destruction is still conceived and effective as an attack on fellow-men.

Ecological Violence

All this is the obvious violence to man and property about which mankind has long been concerned. It is only in the last decade that a less obvious but ultimately much more destructive attack on human 'property' has been discerned. To describe as violence the pollution of the atmosphere, the gradual destruction of it and other essential natural resources by modern technology, can be readily understood. Increasingly we are conscious of the indivisibility of all men and the planet as a whole. No twenty-minute or twenty-year warnings will allow men to evacuate the only planet they have in face of the imminent or gradual destruction of their biosphere, the critical 'property' of all men, without which they cannot survive. Attacks by men on this 'property' are now revealed as a widespread and particularly serious form of violence on one's fellow-men.

Motives of Violence

The men who do violence, directly or indirectly, to their fellow-men are moved by various kinds of motivation. Some of the violence appears to lack intelligible motivation. Arbitrary and aimless personal attacks on or destruction of humans and their goods frequently occur. It is sometimes possible to discern a certain protest element in such occurrences, particularly protest against the social conditions in which the doer of violence finds himself. At any rate the analyst of violence, such as the composers of the *Report of the (U.S.) National Commission on the Causes and Prevention of Violence (1969)*[2] must seek to discover the social and psychological causes of what to all appearances are irrational outbursts of violence. It is far from clear that this or any other commission has accounted satisfactorily for the pervasiveness of such violence. How far it has been complicated if not triggered off by such recent western phenomena as the use of drugs and preoccupation of television with violence is simply impossible to say.

Personal and group violence has always been practised for financial gain. Violent robbery remains a frequent and serious crime. It may be that some people involved in it are more interested in the violence than the gain. They would overlap with the people discussed in the last paragraph. It is customary to think of such robbery as simply immoral and of the personal gain as not justifying any resort to violence. However there has been the Robin Hood tradition of robbing the rich to look after the poor and it is occasionally still invoked to justify a particular incident.

Political Violence

It is political motivation which today is most commonly invoked to justify violence and which in the Christian as well as in the wider tradition of civility has provided man with not only justification but also a mantle of virtue at heroic level for his violent activity. The violence of war (inter-state violence) is still with us in all its crudity and cruelty. The violence of revolution (intra-state) exists or threatens in a score of states. However questionable may be its other effects, war-reporting, above all on television, has left us in no doubt about the horrors and in every doubt about the traditional glory. The limitations on means, by respect for non-combatants and for a certain code even in regard to combatants, have proved very fragile with the development of modern weapons. All war tends to be total war; the only limitations are politically motivated, not ethically. Indeed it was probably always so. The religious wars

2. Published by the *New York Times*, New York 1970.

of seventeenth-century Europe were probably as total as those of the twentieth. Clausewitz[3] was articulating in the nineteenth century a logic of war and violence which was known intuitively to politicians and soldiers long before.

It is scarcely useful to try to distinguish too nicely within political violence. Such distinctions are not usually the concern of the agents of violence. Yet it might be worth drawing attention to the very extensive employment of *torture* for political ends which is happening in the world of our own time. In the liberal democratic west we may naturally think of eastern and communist countries. We can hardly avoid taking notice of the accounts which emerge from Greece or South Africa or Brazil. But then such countries are not democratic or liberal. The evidence from Vietnam can hardly be reassuring for Americans or the evidence from Northern Ireland for some of the rest of us. And these are only a few of the instances involving western countries which could be mentioned.

A distinction between legal and illegal violence underlies much of the discussion of the problem. Violence by the army, the police, prison officers and official executioners which is in accord with the approved forms is presumed legal, accepted and moral, even if accord with the approved forms may sometimes mean no more than being subject to the direction of the officer in charge. Recently established excesses on the battlefront or the street or in prisons should make one cautious about these presumptions. A great deal more attention to modes of violence used by the civil authorities is clearly called for before one can adopt a high and mighty attitude to some of the unauthorised or illegal violence which plagues so many societies.

Institutional Violence

Recalling the thrust of the definition of violence as destruction of or damage to human persons or goods, one has to

3. *Vom Kriege* first published in 1832. In his introduction to the Pelican edition published in London 1968, Anatol Rapoport sees a revival of Clausewitz's 'realistic' attitudes in recent American writing.

recognise that this can be done in an endless variety of ways, of which the physically violent ways form only one category. The physically violent action is physically discernible and so are its effects in terms of a broken nose, lost limb or life or bombed-out building. Yet destruction of or damage to human persons is certainly caused by human agents in ways which are not physically discernible and whose effects cannot be measured in terms of physical injury or damage. The social structure into which people are born and in which they grow up can damage and even destroy them as people. For the development and maintenance of that structure at least by neglecting its reform some people have or had responsibility. The people who suffer helplessly from that structure suffer violence. The people who have the power to alter it are inflicting violence. In the ghettoes of the world, and some of them are practically nation-size, the physical violence to which so many of the oppressed are driven is a reaction to the institutional violence under which they suffer. Unfortunately as Helder Camara[4] has so penetratingly observed, the reaction of the institutionally violent to the oppressed is likely to be more violence and so the spiral develops. In any contemporary discussion of violence, particularly of the political kind, institutional violence cannot be ignored.

Institutional violence will usually be accompanied by legal and illegal forms of physical violence which will escalate in face of resistance. It may become predominantly physical in its manifestations and effects. The 'purer' form, because less obvious and much more pervasive, is usually more difficult to combat and more deadly in its effects in the long term. Closely related at least as imposed by established institutions are forms of violence more directly aimed at the minds of the violated. These can range from the cruder and more sophisticated forms of brain-washing through certain propaganda and advertising practices to education in the 'god-culture' of particular societies. While the institutional violence of the oppressors is aimed

4. *Spiral of Violence*, London 1971.

at protection of their power and privilege and indirectly, through social conditions mainly, impinges destructively on the minds and characters of the oppressed, the mental violence of the other techniques directly attacks the minds of the victims. In its extreme forms it relates closely to torture, although in common usage the political goals differ : for torture the end in view is information or revenge (or sheer sadism); for brainwashing it is transformation of the mind and personality.

To cite educational practice in this connection may seem to be dangerously exaggerating. Yet the distortion of the personality to which the worst educational practices lead and the bias which even the best may encourage reveal how vulnerable the young human is and how easily he may be twisted in school or home. The relation for example between education and nationalism and nationalist wars deserves much fuller investigation and would certainly indicate the close connection between outbreaks of physical violence such as war and the practice of mental violence in distorted education.

A further disputable association between certain therapeutic practices and violence was brilliantly aired in the novel and film *A Clockwork Orange*. Indeed a great many of the themes mentioned above figure in these works. The point at issue here is more sharply focused in the current debate about psychosurgery. How far are such interventions basically destructive of the human personality? If they are not necessarily so, how far could they give the surgeon (and his masters) the power to control people on allegedly therapeutic but really political or other grounds? How far does all this offer a new and powerful means of violence to the person? If it does, it would be very naïve in the light of past and present achievement to think that it will not be used in this violent way. One cannot help feeling that the predominance of a behaviourist psychology and the preoccupation with learning as conditioning provide fertile ground for such practices. Without denying the useful if limited insights which behaviourist theories have to offer, the reductionism of the predominant schools is inadequate to a proper understanding of human behaviour and dangerously open to encouraging exploitation of the weak, the delinquent or the plain dissenter by the established powers. Therapy easily becomes a manner of ensuring conformity. The more obviously violent technique of brain-washing has found a very acceptable substitute.

In discussing the various modes of human violence in terms of subject, object, purpose and means, the question of causes, individual and social, was touched on merely in passing. It would be nice to be able to give a full and informed analysis of causes. That is not at present possible, if it ever will be. The current debate has been greatly stimulated for the layman to these sciences by the ethological and anthropological publications of recent years. The work of Lorenz and Ardrey on animal behaviour and its extrapolation to human behaviour and the further development of this by a psychiatrist Anthony Storr has called attention to the peculiarities of intra-specific human aggression and placed great emphasis on the 'instinct' of aggression.[5] Such extrapolation has naturally been queried by other scientists and indeed the validity of the scientific 'ethological' work on which it is based called in question.[6] As a disagreement between experts, the ethological debate has no place for a theologian. Yet even he must be struck by continuities and discontinuities between sub-human and the human, although their exact definition may still be disputed.

Behaviourist psychologists are likely to find much for their comfort in the ethologist's extrapolations. The psychodynamic school may prefer a rather different and more exclusively human approach to causes of violence in terms of infantile experience and the influence of the unconscious. Sociological theories, independent of or in combination with psychological theories have also been developed in attempts to explain this

5. The obvious and popular works are: Konrad Lorenz, *On Aggression*, E. trs. London 1966; Robert Ardrey, *The Territorial Imperative*, London 1967; Anthony Storr, *Human Aggression*, London 1968. Prior to and subsequent to these books a very large literature has appeared.

6. Some of the more critical articles for example have been collected and edited by Ashley Montagu, *Man and Aggression*, London 1968.

widespread and frightening human phenomenon. The value of all this work in giving a single satisfactory explanation may be doubted. Yet the various sciences bring forward important evidence and insights in a way that suggests multiple and complex causation beyond the scope of any one science and at the same time suggest certain therapeutic and preventive measures at the biological, psychological and sociological levels. At this stage of our discussion that is all that can and need be said.

Fluidity of Terms and Continuity of Realities

A common intellectual weakness in discussing difficult questions today is the fluidity of the terms employed. To employ the word violence to describe such diverse phenomena as acts of war, pollution, social exploitation, certain educational practices and psycho-surgery seems a good recipe for total confusion. In an effort to avoid that confusion it may help to examine fluidity of terms as a common feature of our intellectual world. By fluidity of terms I mean not primarily the extension of these terms to what would previously be regarded as quite diverse phenomena and so might be quite unjustified, but the discernment of certain continuities between hitherto apparently unrelated phenomena and the inevitable extension of the terms. In the sciences such continuities as they emerged were expressed in the hybrids which now form a normal part of our scientific vocabulary in biochemistry, socio-economics and the like. The unity and complexity of the world has forced man to adopt combined approaches to almost every aspect of it. At the level of human existence the unity and complexity reach their highest intensity and call for a combination of analysis and synthesis which is frequently beyond immediate attainment. The environmental challenge serves to emphasise the unity-complexity character of the world and reveals radically new continuities between man and the cosmos. Evolutionary consciousness and the vision in which Teilhard de Chardin embodied it has played a similar role. The network of communications, from Telstar to the Jumbo, which now encircles the globe, has at once provided the technical basis for expressing the continuities and actually created new continuities in experience as well as in the concepts and words in which they are captured.

In philosophical-theological discourse the continuities and associated fluidity have been no less operative. While certain schools have rightly insisted on maintaining precision of meaning for all terms used, in ethical discussions particularly relevant here, words like responsibility, love, sin, have been used in a much more extended way. This has been in a genuine attempt to cope with the newly discovered variety and extension of the reality. However, it has sometimes led to serious confusion and even impoverishment of the terms which it was meant to enrich. Where love is compatible with any kind of human behaviour, critics[7] of a certain kind of 'situation ethics' have pointed out, it becomes a meaningless and empty term. Fluidity and extension of terms based on established continuity of reality and meaning is not looseness or equivocation.

Sufficient continuity has already been established, I believe, to justify the extended use of the term violence proposed. Yet the possibility of confusion remains. The possibility will undoubtedly be exploited for self-interest. Every attempt to enforce the law and protect citizens may be criticised and opposed as 'institutional violence' by the opponent of the established structures. Every violent activity and effect, physical or institutional, done in the name of the established structures may be excused on the grounds of the universal and ineradicable character of violence, for which nobody therefore can be held responsible. The emergence of continuities and the extension of terms in violence as in other human phenomena call for more discriminating use of language and more sensitive discernment of reality, not less.

Focus on Political Violence

For the moral theologian the questions raised by the com-

7. Cf. Paul Ramsey, *Deeds and Rules in Christian Ethics*, New York 1967.

plete range of modes of violence are all important and inter-
connected. In keeping with my own current preoccupations
and in order to chart a clearer way through a tangled field, I
will focus on 'political' violence without ignoring the more
obvious connection with other forms. Even this corner of the
field is quite tangled as the discussion of legal and illegal,
physical and institutional violence has already indicated. Again
in order to simplify discussion I will concentrate more on
physical violence, legal or illegal, by upholders or opponents
of the 'establishment'. This should not, however, be taken as
any indication that the physical is always the primary form of
violence or necessarily its most evil form.

Three Levels of Discussion

In the debate about physical violence as a political instrument, several different levels of discourse tend to get confused.
I would like to distinguish three which are seldom sufficiently
distinguished : the political effectiveness, the ethical evaluation
and what I might call for the moment the deeper significance.
These in turn may require further sub-distinctions but they
do provide a framework for discussion which is frequently
lacking.

Political Effectiveness

Political effectiveness is the obvious suasory force in any
debate about the employment of violence for political goals.
Whatever else may be said about violence, the argument goes,
it has certainly proved itself effective. Almost any modern or
ancient state you care to mention was born either in actual
violence or under the threat of it. It has continued in existence,
if it has, because it could command sufficient physical violence
to defeat or deter its enemies within and without. A third world
war has been prevented and peace or at least the absence
of global violence has been paradoxically achieved by the
development of terrifying instruments of violence and of the
mental willingness to use them in certain circumstances. Witness the Cuban crisis in 1963.

A variation on the argument underlines the ineffectiveness of any other instruments in certain situations. In face of violent physical attack from within or without what other defence is possible? In face of much institutional violence all constitutional, non-violent methods have proved to be failures. The only alternative is physical violence. Similarly, one might be fairly asked the question: what privileged group has ever surrendered its privileges and so ended exploitation except in face of violence or the threat of it? When has that threat been taken fully seriously until violence has actually broken out? How often then have the terrorists of one day become the prisoners of the next and the partners in negotiation of the day after that?

The lines of the argument are easy to develop and instances could be readily invoked from modern and ancient times. Yet it is impossible to be satisfied that the argument is as easily conclusive about all or any of these past instances or that even if it were, it could offer finally valid and compelling reasons for applying the same violent solution to a fresh instance in the present or future. The lesson of history is notoriously difficult to read. Sheer fact is an abstraction, both from the complex web of information which is available in both its data and lacunae and from the personal equation of the historian in his gifts and limitations. On scarcely any issue is the historical assessor driven to conclude that political achievement was achieved exclusively or even predominantly by a particular use of force, still less can he definitively rule out the possibility that the same goals might have been more or less equally achieved by non-violent means. These conclusions rest on a balance of probabilities. How the probabilities are assessed may well depend on the bias of the assessor. Historical judgment, particularly where political commitment is involved, can often be a matter of option. It is no part of my intention to decry the achievement of the historian or to suggest that no firm historical conclusions are possible at all. I simply want to draw attention to the difficulty of establishing the effectiveness or ineffectiveness of certain political instruments. In particular,

I want to examine the use of the historical argument in relation to proposed future political decision. However clear-cut the facts alleged may be for or against a particular means in the past, their interpretation may well be more under the influence of the political decision about the future they are asked to support, than the other way round.

There is one other very important consideration which is frequently overlooked in the argument about effectiveness. How does one measure political success or failure? A particular oppressor (home or foreign) is finally overthrown. Such a conclusion would seem to count as clear success. But would one have to take account of the replacement or of how far the methods used exercise a pernicious influence later in propagating a violence which is then easily used against dissenters from the new regime? Here one is verging on the ethical question, but it serves to bring out again the complexity which a simple presentation of the effectiveness argument so easily ignores and to emphasise again the impossibility of assessing effectiveness divorced from the influence of political commitment and ethical evaluation.

I have listened to a great many arguments for and against the effectiveness of violence as an instrument of political and social change. I have heard historical parallels invoked for what has been happening in Northern Ireland and in many other places around the world. To be specific I have participated in many arguments about the effectiveness of the Irish war of independence born out of the Rising of Easter Week 1916, and the validity or invalidity of applying the parallel to the present I.R.A. activity in Northern Ireland. I dot not think that it would be helpful to rehearse these arguments here. The official and probably majority attitude in Church and state in the Republic of Ireland today is that 1916 and the subsequent war of independence was a good thing and effective but that the campaign of the new I.R.A. cannot justly claim to be in that tradition and is doomed to be ineffective. The difficulties of sustaining this position should not be presumed to be impossibilities. The further difficulties posed by the attitudes of probably the majority of citizens and churchmen at the time of the Easter Rising might not be insuperable either, in defending the previous violence as justified and the present as unjustified. There are significant differences between the two situations as various political and ecclesiastical commentators have pointed out.[8] Northern Ireland, however you assess its origins, exists, and two-thirds of its people will not be coerced into unity. They would seem to be driven further away from any desire for unity by the violent campaign. The meaning of effectiveness is sharply posed here. Allowing for the large degree of institutional violence with physical accompaniments which characterised the state for the fifty years of its existence and recognising the severe provocation which the Catholic minority endured, one has still to reckon with the development of techniques other than violence for fighting such injustice which have been developed in the recent decades and which gave promise of being quite effective on their introduction to Northern Ireland.

So the argument goes on. It cannot and should not be avoided. However it hardly ever convinces a believer or unbeliever in the effectiveness of violence or leads him to modify the historical case on which he rests. The 'effectiveness' debate is not necessarily sterile but it is not conclusive.

The Ethics of Political Violence

Christians and morally sensitive people generally might not be expected to find considerations of effectiveness conclusive anyway. The ethics of violence as a political instrument has gone through a long development in Christian thought, however much influence it had in practice. In the conventional manual of Catholic moral theology, violence was treated solely under the heading of obstacles to 'voluntariety' and was concerned with one or more individuals forcing another individual to perform some activity against his will. A typical example would be rape. 'Political violence' was subsumed under various

8. Cf. Cathal B. Daly, *Violence in Ireland*, Dublin 1973, 40-41.

L

headings but particularly under war and revolution. The conditions for a just war or revolution which had been elaborated in this tradition were highly sophisticated and went through considerable refinement from their first adumbration by Ambrose and Augustine through the classical authors such as Aquinas and Vitoria down to the recent discussions about the possibility of a just war today, given the destructive range of modern weapons. For all its sophistication and the authoritative minds which developed it, the just war tradition bears two large question marks; how far is it a genuinely Christian tradition, given the example and teaching of the founder of Christianity? How far is it a serious moral tradition, given that it has seldom if ever been of practical influence? Both these questions demand serious examination today if the present attraction to political violence is to receive any realistic ethical assessment.

The Early Christian Attitude

The main thrust of the New Testament teaching and achievement by Jesus and his followers as well as that of the Church of the catacombs is clearly opposed to violence as a way of life or of politics. The message and achievement centre around the urgency and universality of the love commandment, the overcoming of evil by love rather than retaliation, the mission of the reconciliation which led Jesus to lay down his life for men who were still his enemies. Alongside this overwhelming example and directive, incidents such as the cleansing of the temple (*Mark* 11:15-18) or obscure sayings about coming 'to send not peace but a sword' (*Matt.* 10:34) remain insignificant. Early Church practice, as evident in refusal of military service, and early Church reflection on it by Lactantius or Tertullian or Origen, reinforced the obvious interpretation of the New Testament evidence.[9] However

9. The early Church writers listed have been variously interpreted. However, I believe the overall teaching is clear enough. It is summarised in Stanley Windass, *Christianity versus Violence*, London 1964, 3-19.

effective later theology may have considered itself in reconciling political violence and Christian life and love, it could not appeal directly to either the New Testament or the early Christians. The difficulty about the Christian origin and Christian justification of the ethic of the just war could be ignored but it could not be simply overcome.

The Just War Tradition

The tradition which began with Ambrose and Augustine emerged in the new situation in which the Church found itself. From being the Church of the catacombs it became in the space of a generation the Church of the basilicas. Those once persecuted by the state became its favourites; a religion outlawed found itself established by law as the true religion. Establishment brought its involvement with the interests and structures of the state and the temptation to a kind of mutual enslavement which frequently accompanies such close associations. Certainly the temptation for the Church to use the state and the state to use the Church has too often proved irresistible to churchmen and statesmen. Augustine proved an early warning with his invocation of the state to deal with the Donatists.[10] The new political context provided the setting in which a Christian justification of violence developed. It does not necessarily invalidate the justification itself which depended on a realistic assessment of the need for social protection and defence of the weak against the marauders. As Paul Ramsey[11] has pointed out in our own time, 'in-principled love' may simply have to resort to violence to restrain the unjust aggressor and protect the weak and innocent. Whatever its immediate source and even if no such Christian basis could be advanced for the just war ethic, it still needs to be evaluated as an ethical project.

10. Cf. Peter Brown, *Augustine of Hippo*, London 1967, 226-43; Joseph Lecler, *Histoire de Tolérance au Siècle de la Réforme, I, Aubier* 1954, 83-8.
11. Paul Ramsey, *War and the Christian Conscience*, Durham N.C. 1961.

The tradition grew in the social and cultural context of the breakdown of the Roman Empire, the emergence of the Carolingian empire, the feudal princes and ultimately medieval Christendom. It was not a period particularly free from political violence. Certain Christian conventions such as the Truce of God had a limiting effect on the violence, but violent conversion under Charlemagne for example, the Crusades and later the Inquisition, revealed how much more Christian belief and practice was modified by violence than was violence by Christianity.

The medieval theological achievement also found time and place to discuss the problem of violence. The just war theory was given its first important elaboration since Augustine, and war figured in the *Summa* of Aquinas under the rubric of sins against charity.[12] Capital punishment and killing in self-defence, which later became associated with killing in just war, also received their modern expression and defence as the classical exceptions to the commandment 'Thou shalt not kill'. It was with Francesco de Vitoria (d. 1546)[13] a Spanish Dominican, that the just war theory received its fullest modern development. His intent indeed was to limit the horrors of war and even if he did not have immediate influence on the behaviour of his political and military contemporaries, he laid the groundwork for the later development of international law with the possibility of preventing or limiting war more effectively.

The just war theory as it was eventually adopted by most churchmen and theologians laid down what appeared very stringent conditions : just war must have a just cause, such as defence against an unjust aggressor (or, according to Vitoria, punishment for violation of international law); it must be undertaken as a last resort, so that all other means must have been tried; the evil which will inevitably follow must not outweigh the good to be achieved; only just means may be used,

---

12. Aquinas, *Summa Theol.* II.II, 40.
13. Cf. *Dict. de theol. cath. XV*, 3117 ff.

a principle which underlay the condemnations once made by churchmen of particular means such as the bow and arrow, and which found more effective formulation in the conventions developed in the nineteenth century dealing with the protection of non-combatants and prisoners of war; war may be declared only by the lawful authority in the state. This last condition would clearly rule out rebellion against the actual authority but the case where the actual authority was tyrannical and no other means of redress existed, was allowed for.

The obvious theoretical gap in such a system is the absence of any impartial manner of assessing how far the conditions were fulfilled. Each man (prince or rebel) had to act as judge in his own case. This, it would be argued, was less a failure in ethical analysis than in social, international organisation. Yet the rejection of violence as a political instrument and particularly the rejection of war were often dismissed as unrealistic. How realistic is an ethical theory whose application in matters of such enormous consequence is left to the judgment of the interested party? All moral decision rests ultimately on the judgment of an interested party. How far did the just war theory help him to see beyond his self-interest? The just cause, last resort and lawful means criteria are open to widely differing interpretations in the concrete situation.

In practice the defender of the just war theory is faced with crucial questions. How far has any war, even in the remote past, from which one can take a certain academic detachment, satisfied the criteria of a just war? Even where the cause might be held to be just, how far was it a last resort? How far were unjust means employed? Did the good effect outweigh the evil? More importantly, how far did any initiator of war consider these criteria in any serious way? And during or after the war how far did ethical or Christian leaders criticise their own side for the inadequacy of the cause or the injustice of the means? The exceptions, those who did so, are so exceptional, that they were regarded as cranks if not as threats by religious as well as political leaders. Bishop Bell in Britain objecting to various goals and means during World War II was very much a lone figure.[14] The Austrian peasant Franz Jaegerstaetter[15] went to his death equivalently rejected by the Church leaders who might have been expected to assess Hitler's wars by the criteria developed over the centuries. In recent times there has been a certain improvement but the Church is still arriving breathless and late, when the difficulties of objecting to the Vietnam war or other forms of political violence have been borne by the few conscientious objectors.

Church leaders have not been so slow to condemn revolutionary violence. The Irish Catholic hierarchy has, in spite of the alleged connection between nationalism and religion, a fairly consistent record in condemning violence. This record is not, however, in terms of condemning establishment violence or war, but violence directed against the establishment, revolution. These condemnations may well have been justified in the light of the criteria for just revolution as indicated above, although the post-factum acceptance of at least one of them (1916-1921) does create difficulties about consistency. Of course the condemnation of revolutionary violence is not confined to the Irish. It has been widespread but usually directed against the 'outsiders', because the Church leaders belonged to the established and threatened nation or race. In face of this experience it would appear that the criterion for a just war taken most seriously by Christian leaders, was that the war should be initiated by the lawful authority. On ethical grounds alone this would appear the least important.

In recent decades the just war theory has been severely criticised as inadequate to deal with the new situation created by nuclear weapons and the possibilities of total destruction. The politicians have not shown themselves greatly influenced by this debate and the theologians and Church leaders are

14. Cf. his criticism of 'obliteration bombing' in the House of Lords in 1944, *Parliamentary Debates (Lords)* 1944, col. 737 ff. Quoted in Albert Martin (ed.), *War and the Christian Conscience*, Chicago 1971.
15. Cf. Gordon Zahn, *In Solitary Witness*, London 1964.

divided and unable to give effective moral guidance.[16] On the revolutionary front there has been a greater readiness by theologians and other churchmen to accept the possibility of just revolution. Faced with either a romanticisation of revolution or the impossibility of it in a situation in which very great oppression and exploitation is occurring, Christians seem to have little positive moral direction to offer. At least it is difficult to see that revolutionaries take seriously the moral criteria available or consider condemnations as anything more than irrelevancies when they do not see them as endorsements of the (unjust) status quo.

The just war theory and its extension to cover the just revolution embodies a long tradition of reflection on the problems of political violence. Yet its limitations in practice, and ethics is about practice, are only too obvious. The riposte that it hasn't failed but simply has never been tried is not convincing. Ethical directives which are never tried or applied, for example to their own side by theologians or bishops, can hardly be treated seriously as prescriptions for practice. It appears that the just war theory has very doubtful Christian antecedents and very limited ethical significance. Its failure to deal with the problem of political violence except in the textbook may mean that the problem has been misconceived. However, one must ask whether the alternative ethical tradition, that war is simply unjust, has proved any more helpful.

The Alternative Tradition

The rejection of war as a political instrument would seem to have solid Christian antecedents. But whether such a rejection was precisely what the early Christians understood Christianity to demand is not so easily settled. The evidence suggests that they saw themselves as rejecting violence totally and not simply war. The influence of this tradition never entirely disappeared. In practice it helped to modify the actuality of war

16. The debate at Vatican II on this subject and the final statement in the Pastoral Constitution on the Church in the Modern World indicate some of the divisions.

as suggested above. At the level of reflection it provoked serious examination of the justification of war. But it was only with a group of Christian humanist scholars in the sixteenth century, among them Thomas More[17] and Erasmus,[18] that the protest against war received a fresh and vigorous revival. In subsequent centuries the protest developed into a pacifism which characterised particular religious groups such as the Quakers. In this century, one of the bloodiest of all, new political instruments of non-violent resistance were forged and the names of Mohandas Gandhi and Martin Luther King helped create a new consciousness of the political alternative to violence.

Recent Developments

A complete ethical assessment of the non-violent positions which have been recently adopted and their historical antecedents cannot be undertaken here. It probably suffices to analyse the central argument against war and/or any use of violence. In modern times certainly the more subtle proponents of this tradition recognise the obvious problems presented by vicious personal attacks on children, women and the weaker people. They also recognise the need for order in society which may demand some coercion. How to protect the weak from vicious attack or generally uphold social order without resorting to force—at least in extreme cases—has never been satisfactorily shown. It may be argued that lawful violence of this kind is vastly overused and so abused and that there should be a definite programme aimed at making it less and less necessary but can anyone totally exclude it as never justified at present? It is not entirely unfair to ask whether one would or should protect one's wife or child by force against some physical assailant. At the domestic level then, violence in defence as a (very) last resort is not excluded by all proponents of non-

17. His attack on chivalric romance in Utopia includes severe satirical criticism of the glorification of war and violence.
18. Cf. *Against War* quoted in Windass, *op. cit.*; *Praise of Folly*, London 1971, 181.

violence. They are much more consistent in their outlawing of war. At this political level they might argue that there are political alternatives for attaining their goals and even for defence against invaders or exploiters. Gandhi and King undertook to establish this in practice and succeeded to a considerable degree. They have the final argument that the evil caused by the war will always outweigh the good sought. Historical precedent might be invoked on both sides but many people are beginning to recognise the validity of their side of the case, strengthened as it seems to be by the destructiveness of modern weapons and by the more acute analysis of the achievements of any war: what kind of political relationships does it establish for the future? What seeds of future hostility and destructiveness does it sow?

For many defenders of political non-violence there is a just violence in exceptional cases for the protection of the weak individuals and the upholding of public order.[19] To admit violence at the domestic level may weaken the claim to New Testament origins which scarcely concerned itself with politics, while it creates a consistency problem if no such exceptions are allowed at the level of inter-group dispute. Apart from consistency difficulties this tradition also shares with the just war tradition the problem of applicability. How many people have tried to apply the ethics and techniques of non-violence? The campaigns of Gandhi and King and others inspired by them are of importance here, but whether they owe their strength to very particular circumstances and very particular leaders it may not be possible to say yet. Neither can one judge their lasting impact on the people and situations for which they were developed.

A Question of Salvation

It is very doubtful if in a concrete situation and with real people, the choice between violence and non-violence can be

19. Cf. G. H. C. Macgregor, *The New Testament Basis of Pacifism*, New York 1954, 11; P. Regamey, *Non-violence and the Christian Conscience*, London 1966, 45.

settled by ethical analysis. I do not mean to deny the value of such analysis. (I make my living from it.) In this area of human living as in all others ethical analysis and argument help men towards civilised living together. And it would be unwarranted to suppose that the inadequacy of ethics in the situation is due simply to the refusal of the protagonists to see reason. Very often they may be blinded by various interests or prejudices but the difficulty seems to lie deeper. Violence or non-violence may be an option, a reasonable option in the sense that either should be capable of reasonable defence, but not a reasonable option in the sense simply of a reasonable conclusion to an argument about politics and morality. There are deeper needs and attitudes at work here as some of the most powerful advocates on both sides have recognised. In old-fashioned Christian terms it is a problem of salvation rather than—or at least as well as—a problem of ethics.

In her recent book, Lelia Khaled, Palestinian guerrilla fighter famous for her hi-jacking exploits, says of her decision to take up arms, 'armed struggle was the way to salvation'.[20] Seventy years earlier, Irish patriot Padraic Pearse was voicing similar sentiments. The Irish people could only be reawakened to its true identity by the shedding of blood. The liberation he had in mind was not just political but went far deeper and for Pearse was expressed in quasi-religious terms to which salvation would naturally belong. Georges Sorel's brief 'Apology for Violence'[21] originally published in the French newspaper *Matin* in 1908 has the same religious and indeed apocalyptic feel. His whole attitude to social revolution involved a belief in the transforming and salvific character of violence.

Fanon's Vision

For the contemporary revolutionary the most powerful expression of this approach to violence is to be found in Frantz Fanon. West Indian by birth, French by education and

20. Lelia Khaled, *My People Shall Live*, London 1973.
21. See Appendix, Georges Sorel, *Reflections on Violence*, E. trs. London-New York 1972, 274-6.

Algerian by adoption, his essay 'Concerning Violence' in the most famous of his works, *The Wretched of the Earth*,[22] provides a classical exposition of violence as a way of salvation for the oppressed and exploited.

Fanon is here primarily concerned with the problem of colonisation and decolonisation.[23] He sees colonisation as the achievement of violence, maintained by violence and yielding eventually only to violence.[24] He understands that achievement in settler-native terms—pairs, each defining the other : white and black, good and evil, persons and non-persons. The life, freedom, level of physical existence and personal identity are imposed by the settler on the native by his superior violence. The desire of the native for liberation and identity çannot be fulfilled by the ordinary constitutional means invented by the settler to keep the native in his place and taken advantage of by the willing accomplices among the natives who indulge in constitutional politics. Only the total violent destruction of the settler will allow the native to find his freedom and identity, to become the 'new man' to which Fanon constantly refers. It is only by this total violence in opposition to settler violence that a new society can be created, in which, again to employ a favourite phrase, 'the last will be first'. For the individual native as well as for the society, the personal experience of violence done to the settler is the way of cleansing and emancipation and self-identification, of salvation. Fanon's argument moves through the effectiveness stage. Quoting from a leaflet of the Front de Libération Nationale, 1956, he agrees 'that colonialism only loosens its hold when the knife is at its throat'.[25] No other means except violence will work. Native violence in the current international situation need not fear the apparent superiority of the settler forces. International public opinion combined with the desires of international finance to

22. First published 1961, E. trs. London 1965, paperback (cited below) 1967.
23. Cf. Fanon, *op. cit.*, 26-7.
24. *Ibid.*, 27.
25. *Ibid.*, 48.

protect its own interests will enable the vastly superior native numbers even with quite inferior weapons to achieve the ultimate victory.

At the ethical level Fanon is rightly scornful of the exploitation of western and religious values in protection of the settler and his institutionalised violence.[26] The truth as supreme value is vested in the people, the native people.[27] They are the truth. Here he is already in the transethical and the central message is of personal and communal liberation through violent killing of the settler. A passage from the tragedy by Aimé Cesaire, *Les Armes miraculeuses (Et les chiens taisaient)* is quoted to great effect to illustrate the ecstatic experience of the native in killing his master and of its salvific effects.

'We had attacked, we the slaves; we, the dung underfoot, we the animals with patient hooves,
We were running like madmen; shots rang out . . . We were striking. Blood and sweat cooled and refreshed us . . .
I struck, and the blood spurted; that is the only baptism that I remember today.'[28]

The totally changed set of relationships or society, the birth of a new species of man, the liberation and attainment of his identity and dignity, the mystical experience of all this in the acts of violence themselves, the blood brotherhood that is born —these constitute the real meaning of political violence for Fanon's revolutionary. It is on these grounds and not the more mundane calculations of a narrowly based political effectiveness or the detached ethical evaluation of just cause or lawful means that he urges the use of violence.

Fanon was explicitly dealing with anti-colonial revolution but he saw this in almost global terms.[29] He thought of his

26. *Ibid.*, 34.
27. *Ibid.*, 38-9.
28. *Ibid.*, 68-9.
29. His writings have acknowledged influence on many people in many places including Americans such as Eldridge Cleaver, see the Introduction, by Maxwell Geismar, to Eldridge Cleaver, *Soul on Ice*, London 1969.

message as applicable around the world. Most of the wars we have or face have a colonialist or anti-colonialist element or can be interpreted to have. The appeal of violence which Fanon so powerfully articulated in this essay has undoubted universality. Elements in it had already been expressed hitherto and the glorification of war which has formed such a consistent part of all national myth and education gave a more discreet expression to some of the elements identified by Fanon. The option for violence has never been simply in terms of political effectiveness or ethical acceptability. A deeper attraction and satisfaction was always also at work. As elaborated by Fanon it may with some justification be called 'salvation through violence'.

Personal Violence and Salvation

The 'salvific' elements which Fanon's analysis revealed apply properly to political violence. I have no doubt that some of these could also be found in the non-political personal violence which sometimes occurs with quasi-religious overtones today. In an unpublished lecture delivered to the Irish Theological Association in January 1973 and entitled 'Salvation through Murder?', Professor R. C. Zaehner of Oxford analysed the Manson murders and pointed out that in his personal life and influence on his disciples Charles Manson communicated an ecstatic sense of killing. For Zaehner the source of Manson's attitude and influence was ultimately some version of eastern mysticism although similar experiences could be induced by drugs and sex. What is relevant here is Zaehner's interpretation of the killings in this religious fashion and the sense of salvation which Manson and his followers evidently derived from violent sex and murder.

Gandhi

Despite the violent realities of the twentieth century which found one prophet among others in Frantz Fanon, new political instruments and their prophets emerged which opened up new possibilities for mankind. The greatest of these prophets was undoubtedly Gandhi.[30] The most powerful of the political instruments proved to be his. Like Frantz Fanon, Mohandas Gandhi was born in one colonial country (India), trained in the mother country and first became politically involved in another colonial country, South Africa. He took up the cause of the Indian and other people there against the racial as well as colonial oppression which they were suffering. During his South African period, 1893-1918, however, he already laid the foundation for his life-style and life-work and in a fashion opposite to that of Fanon.

Gandhi adopted a radical approach to colonial oppression and the ways of overcoming it. He saw it as a destructive relationship, destructive of both sides. For him the mutual enslavement involved must be transformed into mutual emancipation. Salvation must be achieved for both sides. Herein lay perhaps his closest affinity to and deepest separation from Fanon. Both realised the need for total transformation of the present relationship; amelioration of the worst excesses of colonialism or any other master-slave relationship would not suffice. For Fanon the emancipation and transformation would be achieved by the elimination of the master, the settler. For Gandhi it should be conversion, not elimination. His attitude to the British masters of India remained one of respect and love with a firm determination to remove their colonial rule. He saw it in terms of liberation for the British also.

The institutionalised violence of colonial rule and the physical violence in which it so often and brutally expressed itself could not be overcome in Gandhi's view by opposing violence to violence. Even if such violence should result in a change of masters, the violent relationships would be perpetuated. In his awareness of the close connection between end and means Gandhi differed from his political contem-

---

30. The most useful Christian theological analysis of Gandhi I found in Regamey's work cited in note 19 above. His own writings, particularly the autobiography, are now fairly easily accessible. A good selection is available in Ronald Duncan (ed.), *Selected Writings of Mahatma Gandhi*, paperback, London 1971.

poraries and successors. The end is contained in the means. Fanon was espousing the same axiom with very different content in his appeal to the need of experience of violence to ensure personal liberation for the native. As Gandhi insisted, 'if the means and the end are not identical, they are almost so. The extreme of means is salvation. Salvation of the Gita is perfect peace.'[31]

The means for Gandhi was non-violent resistance, described in the word coined in his South African campaign, *satyagraha*.[32] Literally the word means 'firmness in the truth', but it became his word for the various modes of non-violent political resistance to oppression in which he was engaged for most of his life. He distinguished *satyagraha* in attitude and content from simple passive resistance. Again he rejected, like Fanon, the non-violence of the weak or cowardly. *Satyagraha* was only for the strong, the brave, those able to use violence but prepared to renounce it. Prepared is the key-word. He had to confess so often that his people or even he himself were unprepared for the demands which this way of opposing injustice and achieving justice imposed.

The training or ascesis which Gandhi saw to be necessary was verified in his own life and in the greatest achievements of his followers. It bore witness to the spirit of man in a way which made the heroics of war seem truly sub-human. The philosophy at the back of all this included genuine Indian perceptions such as the notion of *Ahimsa*[33] which Gandhi developed in the course of his own 'experiments with the truth'. *Ahimsa* conveys the idea of reverence for all living things and for him combined a cosmic range with a commitment to love of enemies which few Christians could hope to excel. Gandhi acknowledged his Christian debts, particularly to the Sermon on the Mount and the personal life of Jesus.

Fanon and Gandhi offer radically different solutions to

31. Gandhi, 'Commentary on the Gita', in Duncan, *op. cit.*, 35.
32. 'The Birth of Satyagraha', in Gandhi, *An Autobiography, The Story of my Experiments with Truth*, Boston 1957, pp. 318-19.
33. Cf. Regamey, *op. cit.*, 162-7.

political injustice. They are at one in transcending the terms in which these problems are frequently discussed, effectiveness or ethics narrowly understood. Effectiveness and ethics are now transformed on the deeper level which Gandhi and Fanon have unveiled. It is at this level that man must finally choose. It is a choice for every man in some degree and a choice for mankind which is becoming more crucial by the year. I have no doubt that from a human and cosmic point of view Gandhi has signalled the way of growth and ultimate fulfilment, Fanon the way of distortion and final destruction.

Christianity is not primarily about ethics but about salvation. God's gift of himself to man, in the man Jesus Christ who overcame human violence and the fear and hatred of which it is born, by love, is continually seeking expression in the world as a saving force, liberating every man from fear and oppression and violence, reconciling men with one another. The Christian call is to cooperate with this divine gift in its saving activity. Christian ethics searches out the ways and means of cooperating. It may be that in special circumstances a holding operation is all that can be achieved and violence done to individuals or groups has to be forcibly restrained. Yet the individual Christian and the Christian community can only recognise this as a failure to release the divine saving gift and must renew their struggle to let God in his love triumph over the fear and hatred of our oppressive and violent relationships. In the final end to that struggle, the incarnation, the presence of God to man in his fellow-man, will be complete. Every man will now be gift and no longer threat. Love will finally have driven out fear. In the fullness of salvation ethics will be unnecessary.

For the interim, salvation, while still incomplete, reveals the value and limitations of an ethics of personal and political relationships in which forcible coercion may be necessary at times but must always be secondary to the loving and non-violent activity of which Jesus was the master and Gandhi the great modern prophet.

10

Discerning God's Action in
the World

THE title of this chapter underlines in a special way the
difficulties of speaking about God today. In a secularised age
when God-talk is widely regarded as meaningless, discerning
his action becomes that much more difficult than in an age of
faith, when it still presented formidable problems. When God
has for a world come of age become at best an unnecessary
hypothesis or at worst a threat to genuine humanity, attempting to discern his action appears either foolish or dangerously
misleading. It may be said that this is a task for believers only.
It was not an easy task in the ages of belief. Undiscriminating
description of everything that happened as God's action in
'First Cause' terms created enormous problems in understanding widespread evil and suffering of every kind. Discrimination
when it was not a merely 'God is on our side' rationalisation,
demanded criteria which were not readily available. Today's
believer lives in a secularised age. He shares many of the
difficulties of meaningless, unnecessary hypotheses and threats
to human autonomy voiced by unbelievers. His conscious daily
life is lived as if he accepted completely the secular standpoint.
In his worship and prayer he attempts to transcend that attitude but in his analysis of situations, personal and social, from
Northern Ireland to the Common Market, to marrying this
particular partner or buying this particular house, it does not

M

occur to him for the most part, I believe, to consider discerning God's action in his world. Faced with this challenge he would feel that, in order to attempt it, he would need to be able to explain what he was doing to his unbelieving friends, even though he knows that acceptance of an answer implies belief.

This is perhaps a rather elaborate expression of the obvious difficulties of discussing this topic today even for the believer. The banal conclusion that only believers can make sense of the question and so of any answer should, however, be qualified by the need of some of them to explain what they are doing to their unbelieving friends at least to the extent that they make it clear that they share the same world as starting-point. Here we will try to approach the problem from experience of this world which it is hoped will also be intelligible to people who do not share the author's Christian belief, on which he ultimately depends for his understanding of this experience in terms of God's action.

Because it is my professional preoccupation and because it offers for me one valid and central way of viewing human experience, I shall concentrate on the moral dimension of human experience. I have long ago learned that even here there is no one agreed way of describing, structuring or even identifying the moral experience, even among Christian believers. Some people including myself accept a number of ways of identifying and describing it. The one I use in this book is, I believe, a justifiable one and will, I hope, find echoes of assent, if not complete acceptance, among a range of believers and unbelievers. The elements I focus on are undoubtedly influenced by the task in hand, the discerning of God's action in the world.

The Moral Experience

The moral dimension of experience is most clearly and properly recognised by me in the situation in which I individually or as a member of a group have an unavoidable obligation to make some response to another person or group of persons.

Of course what I describe as moral obligations do not always *immediately* concern other persons. But *mediately* at least they concern persons. In obligations to respect 'things', for example, the element of property and so of proprietor or person plays a role. In matters unrelated to a particular proprietor such as natural resources and their pollution or destruction, the concern is ultimately people of a particular time or place or of the earth as a whole. Morality then is a dimension of relationship between people, that dimension which is expressed in terms of obligation or duty or call. Without accepting that there is an ultimate contradiction between a morality conceived in terms of duty and one conceived in terms of goal, I find in my own experience that the duty enjoys a certain primacy and that in the situations which I would characterise as supremely moral, the duty has a certain unavoidable or unconditional quality. It is not an 'if' or conditional demand which one experiences but one without any conditions attached whatever, which one feels obliged to fulfil despite personal dislike or disadvantage. Not every moral situation presents this kind of demand. Some are very conditional or perceived as such, even if a certain unconditional element may emerge on closer examination. And it may be that one is simply unable to discern clearly what one ought to do in the circumstances and so one is not faced by any such unconditional demand. For me it remains true that such unconditional demands when they occur are the clearest expressions of the moral dimension of experience.

I am not concerned for the moment about the very difficult question of how one recognises a particular demand as the true moral one in any situation. The relation between situation and principle/rule/value which has been so much debated in recent times is of immediate interest to me in so far as I believe that the debate has underlined that our morality is ultimately justified as a respect for persons and not for abstractions such as rules, principles or values. And it is the unconditional or unavoidable character of this respect which at once relativises rules in a particular way and gives the moral demand in a concrete situation its own unconditional character.

I should like to dwell a little on this unconditional respect we are called to show persons. It is another way of saying that they demand to be treated as ends and not as means. I accept this as entering into the very constitution of my moral experience, at once making it possible and justifying it. I find that the admirable people and ideals and movements which have emerged in history embodied this fundamental belief. Without it morality loses its distinctive, humanly convincing and even humanly transforming nature. The belief in or acceptance of this respect for persons which seems to me implied in and to make sense of morality cannot nevertheless disguise some very puzzling aspects of this belief in its origins and justifications. Why should persons demand this kind of respect and not animals or trees or stones or machines or works of art? It must be admitted that some people deny any distinction in theory and that all of us deny it in practice from time to time. But why should anybody uphold it? Does an exclusively intra-cosmic set of relationships in any way remove or reduce the difficulty? If in other words man is seen simply as the highest 'product of evolution' we know but still as only a highly sophisticated conjunction of molecules, is our understanding of this respect due to him increased in any way? Or is there here not just a puzzle but a question about a dimension of reality which is not simply intra-cosmic in our usual material and evolutionary terms?

I have found it useful to describe the respect due to human beings which forbids one to treat them as means and so to use them, possess them or eliminate them, in terms of recognition of human otherness. Humans are different from or other than other beings we meet at least in demanding this unconditional respect. More aptly still they are different from or other than one another in the sense that they may not be (and in a real sense cannot be) absorbed by one another through use or possession or elimination. Unlike other cosmic realities which may in various ways be mastered or penetrated or possessed or even destroyed by human (and sub-human) entities in the world, the human being remains and demands to remain finally other than his fellow-human. Attempts to assimilate through possession or destruction refuse to recognise this final otherness and their frequent frustration can be found in the records of family and political history.

Negatively and forbiddingly human otherness presents limits to attempted possession or destruction. Positively and attractively it presents a distinct cosmic centre of knowledge and freedom and feeling, of creativity and decision and relating. This different world is properly accessible through its own free decision. For the human worlds about it this particular one is a mystery to be unveiled. For it is entered by invitation only and the same procedure is demanded from it in entering others.

The positive concept of human otherness sketched here does not mean total dissimilarity. Without communal elements there would be no communication, a factor overlooked by some proponents of 'situation ethics'. The communal and the distinctive elements, biological, psychological, sociological, cultural and historical (or however one chooses to classify them) combine and are combined in a new centre of self-awareness and other-recognition, of self-disposition and other-response. The creative potential of this centre (not always realised admittedly) raises a further question about its closed intra-cosmic origin and fulfilment.

The human being's openness to worlds of space and time beyond itself assumes a particular definition in the moral situation. Openness to the human worlds of the others involves recognition of them in their difference to the point of uniqueness, respect for them in their inviolability and response to them in their particular moral demand. And all of this may be best described as a stage-by-stage moving out of the world of the self and entering the world of the other in recognition, respect and response. It is a self-transcendence which focuses on and reaches out to the other as a world ultimately unknowable and unattainable. The persistent self-transcendence which is called for in the succession of moral situations, whether involving one other or a whole series, never finally attains the world of the other and never finally satisfies the capacity and the aspiration of the self. A question mark hangs over the dynamic capacity to reach out towards the other which is characteristic of man's moral experience.

This outline of some elements in the moral experience is in no way intended as an argument towards accepting the existence of some transcosmic being to be called God or even as the prolegomenon of such an argument. My purpose is entirely different. I wish to draw attention to these elements which may be intelligible (or unintelligible), acceptable (or unacceptable) to other believers and unbelievers, as reflecting something of the human moral experience. I wish to examine them anew in the light of my basic Christian belief in God in the hope of making some contribution to the main task before me here : discerning God's action in the world.

The Christian and the Moral Experience

The elements of 'unconditionality' of the moral call, its relation to the inviolability of the personal other, the creativeness and originality of the personal other, the self-transcendence involved in recognition of, respect for and response to this other, and the questions which all these raise, may not lead to any particular 'world-view'. They open one up to the possibility of discussing 'world-views', including the Christian. In his attempt to tackle the problem of discerning God's action in the world the Christian may use the shared moral experience and its questions to relate that attempt to his own experience and make it more intelligible to others.

In the Christian vision of God as creator and Lord of history who is at once the ultimate source and sanction of the moral call, the call's 'unconditionality' appears to be confirmed. This confirmation leaves one with serious misgivings about the heteronomous character of such a morality and its conflict with human experience and aspiration. The more developed understanding which conceives man as created in the image of God and so distinguished from sub-human creation, which recognises his call to special intimate relationship with God and sees this fulfilled in his call to sonship of God as Father, reveals an inherent and ultimate significance in each man which makes a certain sense of the unconditionality of some moral demands and the correlative inviolability of persons.

Man's relationship to the Absolute we call God, which in its moments of creation and sonship is intrinsic to man himself, confronts the Christian in the moral experience as 'unconditionality' and 'inviolability'. The puzzling character of such human and cosmic aspects of experience is replaced by the ultimate mystery of reality as it is embodied in cosmic and human beings. This can occur without in any way distorting or short-circuiting the human (as too many religious people have been wont to do) and with a greater commitment than ever to respect it because it is only by being fully itself that it can, in the light of Christian belief in the creation and incarnation, embody ultimate reality or God. God's action in the world is discerned in the inviolability of the human beings we encounter and the unconditional moral demands which they make upon us (at least to recognise and respect and so cherish or love them).

The positive potential for creativity which they possess as new centres of knowledge and decision, relationship and communication, reveals the enriching as distinct from the demanding, the gift as distinct from the call, presence and activity of God. In the development of this potential at various levels and in an integrated way, the further divine activity is disclosed. Humanisation, the fuller development of the human potential, expresses in cosmic and historical terms the profound understanding of reality expressed in creation and incarnation. The problem of discerning God's activity becomes in this context the problem of discerning the true direction of fuller humanisation.

The human demand which is made upon one in the moral situation to recognise the world of the other, involves transcending the world of the self to enter this world of the other. The 'by invitation only' access to the world of the other depends on the free decision of the other to unveil and share himself but it is expressed in all the ways in which men com-

municate with one another and not just in these explicit terms.
The personal world as it is encountered is capable of indefinite
further revelation and in its inner being exceeds the grasp of
the recognising subject. It remains for him not just a puzzle
but the mysterious creative centre which he cannot finally possess or control. The relationship which the Christian believes
exists between man in his inner being and the ultimate, never
finally 'graspable' or controllable but always enriching and
challenging and hence mysterious, reality called God, gives a
certain further dimension of depth and understanding to the
human other as one meets him in the self-transcendence of the
moral situation. It is at least interesting to recall a frequent
and distinctive description of the God of Israel as 'holy'
(*qadosh*), as 'the Holy one of Israel'. In Isaiah (in particular)
it has the basic meaning of 'separate' or 'other'. The New
Testament usage of 'saints' for those called to share God's
sonship marks the fullest application of the term to man. And
Rudolf Otto's analysis of holiness in terms of God as the
'wholly other' provides another pointer for us in relating the
otherness of the human which is experienced in the moral
situation and the self-transcendence it involves, to the implications of the incarnation that God is accessible to man in
man. While the incarnation refers specifically to the man Jesus
Christ, the clear import of the New Testament is that through
him the divine sonship is extended to all men. He is the 'new
Adam', head and first-born of the 'new creation', the only-
begotten son but with brothers and co-heirs who enjoy adopted
sonship. So close is the relationship conceived that other men
are said to be branches of the vine which is Christ, members
of his body, sharers with him of the divine nature. And the
recognition and service of the other is recognition and service
of Jesus himself. Discerning God in his active presence in the
world assumes for the Christian in the moral context the form
of discerning or recognising the world of the other. As recognition is a dynamic process beginning with some awareness of this
new world, including respect for it, demanding the response
appropriate to the particular situation and developing in turn a

deeper recognition of the other, the final otherness of God of which the human other is now the mediator makes contact with the recognising subject and is discernible by him in faith.

Because the subject, as I have called him, is also always a human other, the moral situation has a strict reciprocity with mutual obligations of recognition, respect and response, although their concrete expression will normally take differing forms. The moral situation presupposes some communal or shared reality and the recognition of the one by the other is really a distinguishing of other and self. The other-recognition implies at the same time self-identification, the other-respect implies self-acceptance and the other-response implies self-development. In what is primarily a challenge and an activity which centres about the human other and ultimately about the divine other embodied or signalled thereby, there is simultaneously a recognition of the personal value of the self and a development of it. Human morality and Christian belief can come together in appreciation and acceptance of the human self for its own sake and in that deeper understanding of it provided by the doctrines of creation and incarnation. Their mutual support is most strongly revealed in the priority given to recognition and service of the other in identifying and developing the self, both as human and as bearer of the divine. The moral interchange becomes for self and other a realisation of the divine presence and activity and so a means of discerning it.

Moral Experience among Groups: the Christian View

In what has been said so far the reader might easily and justifiably (in spite of a few references to groups) get the impression that the moral experience occurred only between individuals in 'I-thou' situations. In fact very many of the great contemporary moral problems concern large groups of people who cannot be responded to simply as individuals or simply by individuals. All political and much social activity is based on this premise, whether one is dealing with Protestants and Catholics in Northern Ireland, blacks and whites in

Rhodesia or the coal-miners or homeless in Britain. All of these pose group-demand for group-response. All have an undeniable moral dimension. Analysis of such situations in moral terms which would take account of their specific group-character, so that group responsibility, its discernment and fulfilment, and the relation of the individual to it, receive adequate conceptual treatment, has been almost entirely neglected by moralists. I have attempted earlier some analysis parallel to that indicated briefly above in terms of mutual recognition, respect and response with accompanying self-identification, self-acceptance and self-development. Because a group has not a self-conscious centre as an individual has and because one individual belongs to various overlapping groups etc., it is not easy to recognise its distinctive otherness or conceive of its self-transcendence in response. It remains true, however, that the general direction of the correct moral response is other-centred and directed towards greater humanisation.

The Christian attitude here clearly derives from the creation story of man as a social being; the salvation story always dealt with man-in-community so that the key Old Testament figures, Abraham, Moses and the prophets, as well as the key events such as the Exodus and the covenant on Mount Sinai, were figures and events in the formation of a people in whom God's action in the world would be embodied, until it reached its climax in Jesus Christ. And he was the key-figure in the formation of the New People of God which is a sign and realisation of the unity and fulfilment of all mankind. The new Adam by his reconciling death and resurrection, and the communal extension of that through the Church, destroyed the barriers separating men and enabled them to find fulfilment in the universal community of all men called to be sons of the Father and brothers of one another. In this extension of the reconciling work of Jesus Christ which is through community and for community of all men, the reign of God is achieved together with the growth in humanisation, the fuller development of all men in an increasing realisation and sharing of their human potential. In such humanisation the Christian discerns the thrust of God's activity in the course of human history.

Failure and Hope in the Moral Experience

While humanisation is related to other-centred concern directed towards the fuller realisation of the potential of every individual and group in an increasingly unified world, its achievement in the course of history is at best ambiguous. The oppression, fragmentation and frustration from which individuals and groups suffer today seem so widespread and ineradicable that discerning divine activity in growing humanisation is rendered irrelevant. At any rate no discussion of the moral experience can ignore the extensive failure to respond to the call, the extensive rejection in face of response and the intractability of the general human situation which often makes moral effort so painful and so often finally frustrates it in its humanising intention. The failures, rejections and frustrations in Northern Ireland over a couple of generations provide one obvious example of the affliction which touches every man in his personal, family and social life.

I am not concerned with the problem of evil in all its aspects, although they all may be relevant to the problem posed here. In accord with my own interest and point of departure, I am confining myself to aspects which arise in my experience of morality. As I have already indicated, they are my own failure to respond as I know I should in a particular situation, and the consequent dehumanising effect of that; the rejection which I sometimes meet in making the response I feel called to make; the inadequacy of my best effort (individually or collectively) to affect the situation and help the people confronting me; and finally the pain which I sometimes experience in simply abandoning my own self-centredness and recognising and responding to the others as I know I should.

All these experiences certainly render the moral enterprise considerably more difficult to maintain. For some they might even render it impossible or absurd. Yet one feels called to go on. In spite of one's own continuing failure, in face of rejection by others, recognising that one's best may simply not be good enough and conscious of the pain it may cost, one tries again or wants to try again or believes one should try again and certainly admires those who refuse to surrender to the apparently inevitable, who refuse to give up hope. Hope is the key to continuing moral effort in the situations I describe. It is not easy to explain it as a human phenomenon, much less to justify it. It occurs. It keeps one going. Of course there are people who give up hope and opt out physically or psychologically or socially. There are rather naïvely optimistic people who believe that it is all going to be different, that this activity, scheme or revolution will solve all their problems, remove all their failures and frustrations. There are shrewdly calculating people who proceed on the basis of past experience to risk only so much with a view to so much gain; they are not usually interested in humanising; no calculation based on the past is adequate to every situation; for all their care and success they cannot guard against the inevitable and incalculable destruction of death. And there are people, perhaps most people in varying degrees, who realise the difficulties, but in some situations, at least, hopefully attempt to respond.

For them it is not a futile gesture or heroic defiance of the absurd but a genuine desire to recognise and care for the other, accepting the limitations but convinced of the need and the value of trying in spite of them. The hopeful attempt can itself be part of the humanising process but not in any self-regarding, self-satisfied way. The primary concern should be the other and his need, not the self's satisfaction in being able to say 'I tried'. And the source of this hope is not adequately explained by the expectation of success which is earnestly sought but is so often known to be denied through the weakness of the self, rejection by the other or the inherent difficulties of the situation. At the political level different ideologies or visions provide the mainspring for a while but they all eventually have to accept the limitations imposed in history from one or all of these three sources.

There may be here some inarticulate groping for a source of moral significance and moral energy which enables one to carry on in face of all these difficulties but which is not identifiable or even intelligible in closed cosmic terms. At least the phenomenon of hope which is characteristic of the moral experience leaves the moral analyst with a question which moral analysis does not seem able to answer. The answer would again seem to lie beyond moral analysis in terms of one's world-view. It may be that the experience of the question in the moral dimensions will stimulate one to ask the question and prepare one for the answer. If the experience is authentic and the analysis of it correct the answer will have to be consistent with that experience.

In the Jewish-Christian tradition these difficulties have been puzzled over for several millennia. No easy answers are available. Yet that whole tradition in both its old covenant and new covenant phases may be aptly described as the survival of hope based on the gracious acts of God which embody his promises and are a guarantee of his fidelity to them. It is Yahweh who has borne them on eagles' wings out of Egypt, who will according to the covenant on Sinai be Israel's God while they will be his people. The achievements of Exodus and Sinai and the promises they embody provide the framework for the future development of the history of Israel. That development is not any straight-line progress but the crooked-line history of failure and exile which is so well known. The new covenant which is promised in the story and which becomes the Messianic hope of Israel is fulfilled in a no less paradoxical and entirely unexpected way. The background life and above all the death of Jesus of Nazareth appears even by Old Testament standards singularly unpromising material on which to rest the hopes no longer simply of Israel but of mankind. To appeal to the unknown figure who died with other criminals on a cross two thousand years ago as the supreme expression of God's gracious acts among men and his guarantee of their future would be entirely perverse were it not for the completion of the resurrection.

In the risen Christ the Christian rests his hope for mankind and all its enterprise, in particular its moral enterprise. The future of mankind remains open in a finally positive way. The hope which inspires human striving for justice and peace, reconciliation in community for all men and the development of their potential is confirmed and ultimately justified for the Christian in the divine achievement and promise which he recognises in the risen Christ. Personal failure to respond, which could so easily lead one to abandon the struggle and has to be continually overcome in hope, is met by the healing and enabling graciousness of ultimate reality as manifest in Christ. The rejection by the others does not constitute final rejection of self or them for him who has entered into the passion and death of Jesus and his final prayer for forgiveness for his persecutors. The apparent intractability of the human situation, the slow and ever ambiguous movement of greater humanisation and communisation of mankind, the frustrations of the struggle for justice and peace, can find a present significance and ultimate guarantee in the salvation and new creation of the world already accomplished in Jesus Christ and available even now in hope. The hopeful striving for a better world which the moral endeavour represents, enables the Christian to discern the activity of the God of Abraham and Moses and Jesus Christ. The hope phenomenon itself is understood by him and justified for him in terms of the continuing divine activity, and the final validation and transformation of all human effort which it implies.

Agnostics and atheists of various kinds will offer their own justification of the moral enterprise, the call to serve mankind and the open future which lies ahead. And the differences between us will not be settled by any unanswerable argument. Such stances are ultimately not reducible to arguments of the rationally conclusive kind. What has been said here may help us and them to greater mutual understanding as it tries to start from certain shared experiences, although we may deviate in the very terms in which we identify and describe these. There is one last item worth discussing in this context. It cannot in the same sense be called a shared experience because those of us free to discuss it have not personally experienced it. If we had we could not discuss it. It is the inevitable destiny of all of us in death.

Christian hope we have anchored in the resurrection of Jesus Christ, his triumph by the activity of God over death. It is worth relating death more directly to the moral life. At the personal level the value of moral effort is rendered very questionable if after all one's efforts one comes to the same meaningless end, and not only oneself but all the people one has tried painfully to serve. The difficulty is underlined if the highest moral achievement is taken to be laying down one's own life (in meaningless death) for somebody who is only a short time away from the same empty fate. The open future of mankind cannot be shared by the individual or generation that has to make the sacrifices now if death is simply the end. Hope is threatened by the immediate fate which awaits all. Moral effort does not lead to any participation in the final kingdom of peace and justice. Moral activity and much more significantly moral subjects or people may become merely means to this future kingdom to which it is hard to give any meaning except in terms of people; and their meaning has already been relativised in a way that makes the exaltation of the generation to inherit the kingdom (for whom other generations have to be sacrificed) historically very hard to rationalise, ethically very odd and psychologically very unlikely.

In the Christian vision of the future based on the acts of God in the past and the promises embodied in them, death has been overcome in Jesus Christ. The building of the kingdom which, from our viewpoint here, is realised in the moral striving of mankind, has a present meaning. It is a real contribution to the developing reign of God through the humanisation of the world. In Jesus Christ risen from the dead the cosmic and the human were given this final significance. The growth of the kingdom in which human effort is given its deepest meaning and which can demand the most radical personal and structural changes subordinates no one person or generation to any other. In achievement and enjoyment of the final kingdom all persons and generations are offered the grace and call. For the Christian the political stirrings throughout the world which are reacting against injustice, oppression and all the different forms of man's inhumanity to man and are seeking a new set of political relationships more worthy of man and more careful of all men, manifest, if only in a dark manner, the growing reign of God. Here too he discerns the divine activity announced and realised in Jesus Christ. And these stirrings are not subject to the threatened emptiness of death, now that it has been mastered in the same Christ. In the greatest paradox of all, historical death, apparently the end of all man's hopes, provides the gateway to their fulfilment. It becomes the final and most gracious of all God's acts on man's behalf. It is in dying into God's transforming and life-giving love that man discerns most powerfully the divine activity.